THE
COMPROMISING
OF
LOUIS XVI

the *armoire de fer*
and the
French Revolution

Andrew Freeman

EXETER STUDIES IN HISTORY No. 17

First published by the University of Exeter 1989.

EXETER STUDIES IN HISTORY
General Editor   Colin Jones
Editorial Committee
Jonathan Barry   David Braund   Michael Duffy
Robert Higham   Malyn Newitt

Printed and bound by CPI Group (UK) Ltd, Croydon, CR0 4YY

ISBN 0 85989 298 0
ISSN 0260 8628

Contents

Introduction   1

1. Text and Context   9
2. The *Armoire* as Archive   25
3. The *Armoire* and politics   35
   i) The Commission of Twelve   35
   ii) Girondins and Montagnards   40
   iii) Reality and imagery   45

Documents   51

References   101

Acknowledgements

This book grew out of research conducted in Paris and Oxford in 1985. It could not have been written without the generous financial subsidy I received from Balliol College in 1984; I thank John Prest and the other history tutors for their faith and their support. I owe thanks to a number of individuals for their invaluable help at various stages of its gestation and production. My main debt is to Dr Colin Lucas whose constant help I am glad to admit. I am particularly grateful to him for his unselfish sharing of ideas concerning the character of Louis XVI, ideas which focused my own and of which I have made free use in the Introduction. The engravings are from the collection of the West Country Studies Library, Exeter, and are reproduced with the permission of its Librarian, Dr Ian Maxted. Dr Geoffrey Ellis has been a source of enthusiasm and encouragement. Hazel Mills put up with a very frustrated document translator for as long as it took, and has been a constructive, incisive critic. In particular, she helped me sort out the Girondins. Finally I must thank my parents for their hospitality on the front line and for their shared belief in education. I dedicate this book to them, with love.

List of Figures

Figure 1. Satirical print: the discovery of the *armoire de fer*   v

Figure 2. Louis XVI   11

Figure 3. Marie-Antoinette   11

Figure 4. Roland de de Platière   13

Figure 5. Madame Roland   13

Figure 6. Locks (from the *Encyclopédie)*   22

Figure 7. The Trial of Louis XVI   34

Figure 1. Satirical print: the discovery of the *armoire de fer*

Introduction

Literally translated, '*armoire de fer*' means cupboard of iron, or iron chest. In November 1792 an iron safe was discovered in the royal palace after the man who had built it on the King's orders went to the authorities and told them of its existence. The man, a blacksmith named Gamain, did not know what the safe contained, but upon opening it was found to be full of documents. For opponents of Louis XVI, the timing of the discovery could not have been more fortunate. The monarchy had been violently overthrown on 10 August 1792, and the issue of the King's fate lay before the new legislative chamber, the Convention. From the start, it was widely assumed that the documents in the *armoire de fer*, documents which, after all, had been furtively hidden away, would prove to everyone's satisfaction that Louis had betrayed the Nation by working against the Revolution and planning a return to the ancien regime.

Before the detailed contents of the papers had been established, the Convention moved ahead with the decision that it could undertake the King's prosecution. It was confidently believed that the *armoire* contained enough evidence to ensure that Louis would not be found innocent of the general and specific crimes with which he was to be charged. Moreover, the *armoire* was to provide only part of this evidence.

It comes as a surprise, then, to discover that the *armoire de fer* was hardly mentioned during the trial of Louis XVI, despite the use by the prosecution of several of the documents found in the safe. It will be shown below that the *armoire* had more of a symbolic than a practical importance in damaging the King's reputation, and that his Jacobin prosecutors were quite content to shroud the whole episode of the *armoire*'s construction, contents and discovery with a layer of mystery that discouraged further investigation. It is as if the very existence of the *armoire de fer* were enough to compromise the King in the eyes of public opinion, and that it did not matter what the documents it contained actually said about Louis's attitude to the Revolution.

There is a strong sense in which such an account fits neatly into the strategy of any prosecution involved in a patently political trial, particularly where the defendant is a deposed King. The need to establish a connection between the King as an institutional figure and as a person necessarily overrides any possibilities that specific pieces of evidence do not fit easily into a general deposition. It will be argued that the *armoire de fer* was, by its nature, a very personal project, closely connected with how Louis perceived his role during the Revolution, and reflecting his attitude both to events past and to possible outcomes of the contemporary struggle for stability. But all this did not concern the Jacobins on any complex level. They were able merely to infer that the *armoire* proved that Louis was, and had been, anti-revolutionary. This inference took its place as part of the wider case against the King, and the *armoire de fer* went into the history books as the source of the crucial proofs which sealed the fate of Louis XVI.

The consequences of this 'history-making' have been several. First, as this book is primarily intended to show, there has been widespread and fundamental misunderstanding of the *armoire de fer* itself. This misunderstanding extends not only to the events and persons surrounding the construction and discovery of the *armoire*, but also to the nature of the documents it contained. By failing both to look at the documents, and to ask why Louis chose to preserve them, and not others, historians have missed an opportunity to see the *armoire* as a coherent archive. Second, and closely related, this failure has reinforced the traditional views of Louis XVI as a King (which will be examined below). While many aspects of the Revolution have undergone scrutiny and re-interpretation in recent years, the character of the King has remained resolutely cast. Although this has occasionally led to rather unsubtle historical explanations, no-one has seen fit to re-examine Louis in the light of the evidence. In the space available in this book, it is not possible to fulfil this much larger task; nevertheless, it is hoped that the 'case of the *armoire de fer*' will strengthen the growing feeling that Louis XVI may have been seriously under-estimated both as a man, and as a participant in the Revolution.

Louis XVI and the Revolution

It is often noted that history tends to be presented in terms of the characters and actions of 'great' men and women, at the expense of ordinary people. However, recent historical work has widened this traditional focus, to look at society and culture, and to consider how these structures might be understood. The lives of prominent citizens can be scrutinised for common 'threads', lines which link them with their communities or their nation. The historiography of the French Revolution is full of biographical studies of colourful, tormented characters who influenced events and opinions, whose dilemmas encapsulated larger contradictions, and shed light on contemporary concerns. In spite of his central position in the events of the French Revolution, Louis XVI has remained a shadowy historical figure. Perhaps precisely because many historians have argued that Louis was not in a central position, and that the Revolution was an inexorable process in which individuals could play only symbolic roles, the quiet figure of the King, with his hesitant and circumspect approach to the business of ruling, has been relegated to the sidelines. If he is seen as of any importance at all, it is usually as an epitome of the ancien regime, a symbol of everything that had to be overthrown to make way for a new social order. The historian trying to assess Louis faces a historiography full of contradictions. Louis was a martyr and a sinner, a hero and a fool, a reformer and a reactionary. The only agreed opinion seems to be that he lacked good advice and political insight.

It would be easy to think in terms of reconciling the opposing views of Louis's historical judges. It seems to me, however, that the best way to approach him is not through the tangled lines of biassed history; rather, he must be considered in the light of primary evidence. This is a rather obvious statement, but it needs to be stressed, for there has been a remarkable reluctance on the part of historians to try to see Louis through the original sources. This book represents only a partial attempt to re-think his character, and in particular to cast new light upon his political character. It looks not so much at documents he wrote himself, but at documents he kept and sometimes annotated, and it attempts to suggest ways in which our understanding of the Revolution itself might be enriched by a better knowledge of the King. What we conspicuously lack is a reasoned account of the political choices Louis actually faced during the Revolution.

Before proceeding to elaborate this argument, however, it is necessary, if only briefly, to address the question as to why Louis should have been subject not only to historical neglect, but also to extremes of historical judgement that would not be tolerated in many other areas of study. The answer lies in the fact that Louis's kingship, his very status as monarch, overrode his independent identity as a man. Indeed, one might sum up the typical pictures of the King as being drawn from a stencilled outline in pencils of different colours. Both sides of the political spectrum present images of a monarch rather than a man. The difficulties of assessing the man are passed over in favour of the ease with which the institution he represented can be praised, or vilified depending on one's beliefs. Facets of his character which may have endeared him to ordinary citizens, became liabilities in the context of the violent politics of the Revolution, when Louis had to fight as the assumed champion of a whole political culture.

As Tocqueville later pointed out, it was ironic that of all French monarchs it should be Louis XVI who suffered for his efforts to modernise the state of the nation, when he was the only one who made real inroads into the structures and practices that defined the society of the ancien regime. Louis's major problem was that after the beginning of the period of economic crisis that sparked off the political reaction of 1787–89, various groups with conflicting interests claimed him as their own. As a King, he could not endorse the aspirations of the Third Estate and at the same time condone the Declaration of the Princes of the Blood. Later in the Revolution, he was successively abandoned by the same groups which had been so keen to enlist his support in 1789. He could not escape the association of the Crown with the discredited aristocracy, nor the powerful consensus of much of that aristocracy that he had abandoned the responsibilities incumbent upon him as monarch towards his natural social and political allies. Thus the ironic position was reached whereby Louis was condemned on the one hand for being too reactionary and on the other for being too revolutionary.

The idea that Louis was a stupid man has permeated the historiography. In terms of his policy during the Revolution, for those on the 'Right' he was stupid because he gave way to the thoroughly unreasonable demands of the Third Estate, and watched over the demolition of traditional society and the persecution of the clergy and nobility. For those on the 'Left', he clung foolishly to the remnants of the ancien regime in a doomed attempt to check the progress of social equality and political rights. Moreover, these judgements served only to confirm the earlier belief that Louis was not made of the stuff of Kings. Throughout his childhood and adolescence, he was a repressed and silent person, speaking only when it was encumbant upon him. He had a strained relationship with Louis XV. The old King had been shattered by the death from tuberculosis of his gifted eldest son, Louis Duke of Burgundy, in 1761, and found it hard to acknowledge his new heir. After his marriage to Marie-Antoinette in 1770, Louis's reputation was further damaged by rumours of the couple's failure to consummate their union.

This apparent lack of manliness on Louis's part joined his taciturnity as the basis of questions about his potency as a future King.

Perhaps the main source of the idea of Louis's stupidity, however, was the faction of the duc de Choiseul. Court politics at the end of the ancien regime were dominated by the struggle for patronage and the King's ear. The dismissal of Choiseul from office in 1770 set the scene for a realignment of factions after years of domination by the duke and his clients. Louis was the victim of Choiseul's efforts to win back the influence he was accustomed to wielding. In order to persuade Louis XV that his heir would need the guidance of experienced ministers when he came to the throne, Choiseul and his supporters who remained at court gave impetus to the rumour that the young prince was a dullard. The fact that Louis XVI turned elsewhere for advice when he ascended the throne in 1774 only proved their point—how could he ignore the weight of wisdom and experience offered by the exiled Duke, if not through stupidity? Louis was thus type-cast in a fashion made even more damaging by the close relationship between his wife and the very group which sought to undermine him. Her foolish flirtation with the 'Choiseulistes' appeared to lend support to their claims, particularly as she made no effort to deny that her husband was slow. In such a context, Louis's other slowness, that of consummation, took on a damaging significance to that it already possessed.

Yet Louis appears to have been far from stupid. Ideologically motivated historians have failed to explain how a man so unsuited to the complexities of ruling could have been so busy plotting the downfall of the Revolution with all the cunning and deceit of a seasoned political survivor. Those who knew him well, like Malesherbes, the chief defence lawyer at his trial in 1792, characterised him as self-effacing and unsure of his own judgement. The problem was not that he could not understand events and political manoeuvres, but that he found it impossible to make quick decisions on the basis of the information he had received. He liked to move slowly and deliberately, to seek the advice of trusted ministers, and then to embark upon a considered course of action. In the context of the Revolution, this was a fundamental flaw in his political character—it is true to say that Louis reacted too slowly to events as they unfolded, so that his decisions often exacerbated rather than alleviated the situation.

It is very rare for historians to acknowledge that the decisions offered to Louis XVI during the Revolution were difficult, or to explore the idea that he followed a consistent policy or line of thought. Clearly he found the rapid progression of events in 1789 extremely hard to comprehend. He was not alone in this. But he was peculiarly alone in standing at such an influential position. What he did, or desired, was crucial to the process of national regeneration of which he wanted to be the guiding hand, not the obdurate obstructor. The documents examined in this book suggest how seriously Louis took his role, and how difficult he found the balance of change and custom. He wanted reform, but he refused to sanction illegal measures in order to achieve it. He defended religion from what he saw as unconstitutional persecution. He accepted that his personal power would be diminished by the people's participation in politics, and seems genuinely to have desired a constitutional settlement. Above all, he retained a strong faith in the affection felt for him by his people, an affection he reciprocated. If he resented the revolutionaries, it was primarily because they sought to alienate him from his subjects, to cut him off from the body politic. Hence his anger at his trial when he was accused of having spilled the blood of Frenchmen—'Non, Monsieur, ce n'était point moi ... '

In other words, he remained profoundly a King. It was this, more than anything else, which defined his role and policies during the Revolution. Further, like Charles I in England, the disaster of the Revolution allowed him to play the role expected of a King only when it was too late. Until his trial, Louis dithered and worried while the course of events slipped out of his control and the personalities who mattered ceased to consult him. Yet during the last few months of his life, it seems as if Louis had finally come to terms with the demands of his position. In prison, he read histories of the life and death of his English counterpart. It is hard not to speculate that he found inspiration there to act out the drama of his execution. Spectators remarked on the calm courage of the King on the scaffold, in the same way that the English crowd is said to have groaned as Charles's head was held up. There is a supreme irony in all this. As a man who had struggled for so long with the symbolic and practical roles of Kingship, Louis managed at the last to reinforce the power of precisely these things, thereby unwittingly providing the image of the martyred saint which supported so much propaganda. By dying 'like a King', he played into the hands of the revolutionaries, whose rhetoric was given foundation in the popular mind; and into the hands of the émigrés, whose implacable opposition to the Revolution and to the moderating efforts of the dead King could be re-defined along new and plausible lines.

Louis XVI and the armoire de fer

One of the more curious aspects of the period between the discovery of the *armoire* on 20 November 1792 and the execution of Louis XVI on 21 January 1793, is the extent to which the principal actor was absent from the historical stage. Imprisoned in the Temple, confined to two brief appearances before his judges, and keeping a dignified silence, Louis was forced to watch as his fate was decided, and his reputation and probity were debated and denounced.

For over two months after his fall from power, Louis's precious *armoire* remained undiscovered. A more ruthless, or more careful, King would have ensured that no-one but he knew of its existence. Unless they had ordered the dismantling of the entire fabric of the Tuileries Palace, the Jacobins would never have stumbled upon it. But Louis's secret was shared by an ex-servant who hesitated only long enough to be certain that the monarchy would not be restored, before disclosing the location of the *armoire* to his new masters.

It is not clear when Louis himself heard that the *armoire* was open; we can speculate, however, that the news can have done nothing to lift his spirits. He must have known when he conceived the idea early in 1792 that to build a safe at a time when his motives were suspect and his position tenuous, was to take a considerable risk. Such a risk could be justified in one of two ways. Either the safe was intended to hold documents which were so potentially dangerous to Louis and his cause, that they simply could not be kept any other way. Or else the emphasis was more on the safe than the contents, in the sense that the latter needed storing in safety because they were important, rather than in secrecy because they were incriminating. A brief look at the documents which Louis did put in the *armoire de fer* shows convincingly enough that their character does not support the first suggestion. If there was any correspondence with the potential to destroy Louis's credibility, he did not keep it in the *armoire*. He probably did not keep it at all. Evidence given below strongly suggests that the *armoire* was conceived of by Louis as a response to his perceptions of the development of the Revolution, and not because he merely had secret letters he wanted to hide. That is to say, the thought that went in to the construction of the *armoire* was undoubtedly more sophisticated than generally assumed by historians.

It is important to state at the outset that such argument is meant to stimulate thought. It is not intended in any sense to be a 'final word'. The character of Louis XVI will remain elusive until a more detailed study based on primary evidence is undertaken. The purpose of this book is thus twofold. Firstly, by re-thinking the *armoire de fer* and the central role played by Louis in its history, one small aspect of the French Revolution can be brought into a clearer focus. Secondly, and perhaps more profoundly, by examining the myths rooted in the historiography surrounding the *armoire de fer* and suggesting how these myths came into being, it is hoped that something can be revealed of the nature of history itself. In this instance, the historical subject is inescapably political—what one believes is fundamentally defined by allegiance, and by the presentation of the evidence. It would not be going too far to say that this is a lesson which has deep relevance in our society today. Notions of secrecy and concealment lie at the heart of the revolutionary debate on the *armoire de fer*, just as they do in our debate on freedom of information and government accountability.

1. Text and Context

In keeping with its obscure origins, the *armoire de fer* is surrounded by mystery. Its story as told by several notable historians is vague and unlikely. For one standard source, 'the discovery at the Tuileries of the secret *armoire de fer*, containing the royal correspondence with Austria, was the death warrant of Louis XVI' (Cobban 1963, vol.1, p.210), while another evokes 'the iron chest in the Tuileries with its damning disclosures of the King's dealings with the émigrés' (Goodwin 1965, p.709). More recently, a French historian has written that 'in this secret cupboard, put in the wall of a corridor by the locksmith Gamain and Louis XVI, the King kept in particular his correspondence with other sovereigns and his émigré brothers' (Bouloiseau 1972, p.64). In his book *The King's Trial*, David Jordan quotes from a letter which he says was found among the *armoire* documents, written by Louis to his secret adviser the Baron de Bretueil, in which he describes the Constitution as 'absurd and detestable' and says that it makes him 'less than the King of Poland' (Jordan 1979, p.73). In the latest biography of Louis, it is claimed that the opening of the *armoire* revealed 'that Louis was negotiating secretly with Austria and that he had launched a vast network of corruption in the world of revolutionary politics' (Lever 1985, p.647). In all cases these descriptions are misleading and inaccurate. The *armoire de fer* contained no documents which indicated that Louis was in furtive contact with either the émigrés or the Austrian court. The letter quoted by Jordan was not found in the *armoire*, while Lever's claims remain largely unsubstantiated.

It is easy to reconstruct the route by which this fallacious position has been reached. Historians such as those above have relied heavily on the memoirs of several of those involved in some way with the *armoire* either during the period of its construction or subsequent to its discovery. For example, one of the royal ushers, Francis Hue, gave the most detailed description of the *armoire* itself. 'Motivated by prudence, the King decided to build a secret depository in his palace' (Hue 1860, pp.399–400). A site was chosen in a corridor between Louis's bedroom and that of the Dauphin, and Louis himself used a boring tool quietly to cut out a section of the panelling of the wall measuring 22 inches high and 16 inches wide. He then excavated a hole of the same dimensions but about 8 or 9 inches deep. Working each day, he would remove and then replace the panel. Plaster brackets were made to hold two wooden shelves. Finally a locksmith, doubtless Gamain, who was to play a key role in the revelation of the *armoire*, was called to strengthen the panel with a sheet of steel. Louis was then able 'to keep in safety his most important papers'.

Hue's account is at once detailed and vague. He wrote after the event about episodes he may not have witnessed. For example the description of the *armoire* could easily have been obtained by visiting the site after the Revolution. It is unlikely that Louis was so active in the construction of the *armoire*, despite the fact that his interest and skill as an amateur locksmith were well known. The process Hue describes would have taken a long time to complete when presumably Louis was in a hurry.

Madame Campan, Lady-in-Waiting to Marie-Antoinette, also recorded the building of the *armoire*. In order to hide some of his 'prodigious quantity of papers' Louis had the *armoire* built (Campan 1821, pp.222–4). So skilfully was it disguised that it would never have been found but for the locksmith's later treachery. Madame Campan went on to tell an extraordinary story. Marie-Antoinette learned that the locksmith trusted so completely by Louis was a Jacobin. She informed Louis and persuaded him to make up a file of 'all the papers which he particularly wanted to preserve'. Louis not only agreed to this, but also to his wife's suggestion that these papers should be entrusted to Madame Campan. The papers were duly carried to her apartment by the King himself. When she asked her mistress what the file contained, she was told that it included all the documents which would be the most damaging to the King 'if they go so far as to put him on trial'. One document was specifically mentioned—the minute of a meeting of the Conseil d'Etat in which 'the King expressed his views against the war'. It seems curious that the Queen should be contemplating her husband's trial before the monarchy had been overthrown; nevertheless a document such as the one mentioned might have been useful to Louis, if only as insurance against the war going badly. Bearing that in mind, it is inexplicable that he did not hold onto it for himself—it was never recovered

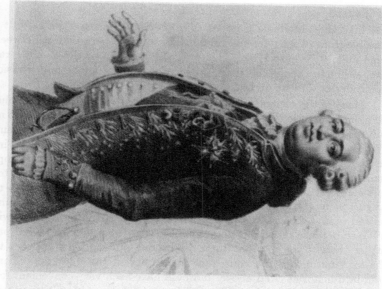

Figure 2: Louis XVI

Figure 3: Marie-Antoinette

for his trial.

Like Hue, Madame Campan is imprecise in terms of dates, but it is possible from other references she makes to place her account between 20 June and 10 August 1792. This puts the building of the *armoire* rather late, although she implies that Louis had decided after the first invasion of the Tuileries that he needed a secret place for his papers.

Many of the memoirs written in the ten years or so after the Revolution were sensationalised in order to satisfy public curiosity, and perhaps to make a dull story more interesting. Former royal servants like Hue and Campan were polemical writers concerned to enlarge or justify their own roles in the last years and months of the monarchy. Thus it is hard to believe Campan's claim that a large file of the most significant papers was entrusted to her sole care; yet it is possible, even likely, that in the days leading up to 10 August papers were destroyed by Louis—thus, no-one could refute Campan. Indeed many of the supporters of the Revolution would not have wished to do so because they preferred to believe that there had been vital papers rather than to accept that there were none at all. This appears to be the explanation for the consistent inaccuracy of the line adopted in the standard histories cited above. It would have been very convenient for the revolutionaries if Louis's dealings with the émigrés and foreign powers had been exposed in the *armoire*. By a sort of historical wish-fulfilment, it has been similarly convenient for historians to believe that they were.

Unlike the other memoirs quoted, those of Madame Roland (wife of the Minister of the Interior, Roland de la Platière, who opened the *armoire*) were apologistic rather than sensationalist. She was determined to show that there was no justification for the charge that her husband had removed some of the documents he had found in order to protect friends who might otherwise have been compromised by the revelation of their dealings with the crown. She argued that Roland had been completely within his jurisdiction when he followed up the claim of the locksmith Gamain. Accompanied by the Inspector General of National Buildings, Heurtier, to whom Gamain's denunciation had originally been made, Roland and Gamain went to the royal apartments in the Tuileries Palace. In a corridor between two bedrooms, Gamain lifted a wooden panel to reveal an iron plate. Roland ordered him to open it. Behind they found bundles of papers stuffed into a hole. Roland immediately called for a servant to fetch a briefcase so that the papers could be removed to the Convention, and during the delay he examined the bundles, the titles of which 'indicated correspondences with the Generals and others' (Roland 1821, vol.2 p.245).

Madame Roland did admit that alongside the Minister's jurisdiction of the Tuileries Palace, the Convention had authorised a commission, the

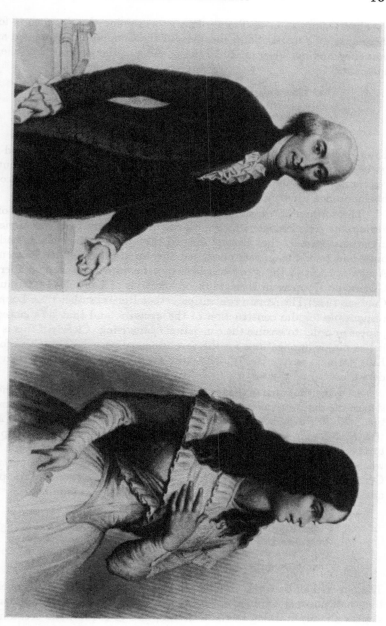

Figure 4: Roland de la Platière

Figure 5: Madame Roland

so-called Commission of Twenty-Four, to examine the documents found there after 10 August. Some members of the Commission expressed anger that they had not been called to the opening of the *armoire*; but she was adamant:

> After Gamain's denunciation, the Minister thought it best simply to visit the site. Having discovered the papers there, he immediately took them before the Convention. He conducted himself as an honest and unsuspecting man.

Later she gave a more balanced comment when she acknowledged that he had made 'a mistake in his conduct and his lack of caution', but she reiterated that Roland's hasty and careless procedure was ample proof of his innocence (ibid. p.247).

The sources above contain the essential elements of the story of the *armoire de fer*, elements which until recently have not been questioned by historians: namely that Roland opened the *armoire* which Louis had had built and took the papers contained therein straight to the Convention. A new version of the story has been put forward by Paul and Pierrette Girault de Coursac in their work on the trial of Louis XVI. (Girault de Coursac 1982) Their main contention is that Roland rather than Louis was responsible for the construction of the *armoire*, and that he planted the papers in order to ensure the conviction of the King. Clearly if this is true, it has major implications for the revolutionary period 1792–3 and for the King's trial in particular. It is therefore worth examining this claim in some detail.

Denying the value of the traditional sources, the authors review the version of the discovery as it emerged in Roland's exchanges with the Convention. On 20 November 1792, Roland appeared in the Convention. (*Moniteur* No.327) He said that he had just brought several bundles of papers to the chamber, papers which 'by their nature and in view of the place where they were found, appeared to me to be of very great importance'. Commenting that the papers might throw new light on some of the people and events of the Revolution, Roland said that he had found:

> letters from Mr. Laporte and several other people attached to the King. There are even original letters in the hand of the deposed King, as well as a large number of plans relative to his Guards, his Household, the Armies and all sorts of schemes to do with the Revolution.

The papers had been so carefully hidden in a secret place that he believed they had unusual significance; hence his decision to by-pass the commissioners already working in the Tuileries, and to request the creation of a new commission to examine the documents. Roland added that he had had the safe opened that morning, and he admitted that he had 'rapidly looked over the papers'.

But what he had hoped would be a major political coup quickly became an embarrassment for Roland and his allies. A Montagnard deputy, Goupilleau de Montaigu, attacked the Minister for what he alleged was a serious breach of procedure. Whilst he accepted that Roland had been commendably vigilant in finding the *armoire* and its contents, Goupilleau protested that he had deliberately ignored the presence in the Tuileries of the Commission of Twenty-Four, whose members were making an inventory of papers found in the royal apartments, and had been working close by when the *armoire* was discovered. Why had Roland not informed them of the discovery? (*A.P.* Vol.LIII p.493-4)

Roland asked for, and was granted, time to justify himself before the Convention. He appeared at the bar of the house the following day. Commenting on the interest all Paris was showing in the affair, he ridiculed those who had denounced his conduct. He described the various accusations against him:

> It is claimed that I should have minuted the papers; that I should have been accompanied by Commissioners of the National Convention when removing them from their hiding place; it is even claimed that there were jewels hidden with the papers, and that doubtless I have conjured away these jewels... (*Indignant reaction*)
> Several voices: Marat said that!! (*A.P.* Vol.LIII p.511)

Roland then stated categorically that he had found only papers, and that he had two witnesses to prove it. Indignantly he asked whether he was expected to respond to the slightest rumour by running to the Convention to request the nomination of commissioners. The majority of the deputies agreed that he was not, and the Minister was applauded as he left the Convention hall.

But Roland was clearly rattled, and on 1 December he obtained testimonies from the two men who had accompanied him when the *armoire* was opened on 20 November. Their statements were designed to corroborate Roland's story to the Convention. For the Girault de Coursacs, however, they contain vital clues as to what really happened. (Girault de Coursac 1982, p.79-80) The first witness was Gamain, the locksmith, who declared that in April of that year he had been approached by Louis XVI and asked to build a cupboard with an iron door 'closed by a security lock', in a passage in the Tuileries palace. Gamain went on to say that on 18 November, he had informed his superior, Heurtier, of the existence of the *armoire*.

Summoned to Paris, he took Roland and Heurtier to the Tuileries on 20 November and showed them where the *armoire* was hidden:

> I opened the door protecting the safe in which the Minister found the documents. He had all these packed up in the presence of citizen Heurtier and myself, so that they could be carried to the Convention by people he had summoned for this purpose.

Heurtier corroborated Gamain's evidence and added that the papers found in the *armoire* had been in his sight from the moment of their discovery to the moment when they arrived at the Convention. He said that the order in which they had been found 'was not even disturbed'.

The next piece of evidence is a letter Roland wrote to the Convention on 22 January 1793. (*A.P.* Vol.LVII p.601) After months of increasing political pressure from within and without the chamber, he decided to resign his ministry. The bulk of his letter referred to other issues such as his attitude to the domination of France by Paris; but in a post-script to the letter, he chose to defend himself for the last time against the repeated charge that he had used the opportunity of opening the *armoire de fer* to destroy evidence compromising to his Girondin friends. Adopting the tone of an innocent maliciously accused by enemies who had no other issue over which they could smear his name, Roland gave a concise vindication of his conduct on 20 November. He said that he had learned of the *armoire* only on the journey to the royal apartments, and that having found the papers he had had time only to organise their removal to the Convention before his own appearance there. Reminding the Convention of the testimonies he had obtained from Gamain and Heurtier, Roland added that 'my swiftness proves that I neither wanted, nor was able, to remove anything'.

This appears to expose a major contradiction in Roland's testimony. Whereas on 20 November, he claimed to have 'rapidly looked over' the papers, he now claimed that he had had no time to read them but had taken them straight to the Convention. 'The fairly precise analysis he gave of them leaves no doubt as to the accuracy of the first statement'. (Girault de Coursac 1982, p.81)

A second contradiction posed by cross-checking the sources concerns Gamain. A special Commission of Twenty-One was organising the gathering of evidence for the King's trial. Two of its members, Bolot and Borie, were sent to the Tuileries to examine five keys that Louis XVI had given to his valet Thierry on 12 August, just after the overthrow of the monarchy. On 24 December, Bolot and Borie took the keys to the royal apartments where they were guided to the location of the *armoire de fer* by one of Roland's staff, Larrivée. They examined the cupboard, and found that it had no lock on it. Larrivée told them that the lock had been forced off on 20 November when the *armoire* was opened, and he arranged that the commissioners would be shown the lock in the presence of Gamain the following day.

Bolot and Borie returned to the Tuileries the next morning. Larrivée showed them a lock which Gamain recognised as the one he had fitted to the *armoire*. The commissioners put it into its place on the door of the *armoire*, and agreed that the fracture lines caused by the forcing of the lock matched perfectly. They had no doubt that this was the original lock. They then tried the keys, and found that the fourth key 'easily opened the *armoire* in question'. But the purpose of their visit to the apartments was to make a general check of the keys and locks, and they found that the key to the *armoire* 'also opens one cupboard in the former King's small office, and two wardrobes in his main office'.

The fact that the key to the *armoire* also opened three other locks means that it was a 'master key' and therefore incapable of opening a 'security lock'. 'The door of the *armoire de fer* was therefore fitted with an ordinary lock, like the cupboard and wardrobes in the King's rooms'. (Girault de Coursac 1982, p.82) Why then did Gamain testify that he had fitted the *armoire* with a 'security lock' when he made his statement on 1 December? Why also did he go to the trouble of breaking off the lock on 20 November, when an 'ordinary lock' would have been easy to pick?

The Girault de Coursacs give a brief summary of the *armoire* papers. They conclude that it is unlikely that Louis XVI would have gone to the trouble of constructing so secret an *armoire* only to fill it with such unincriminating papers, particularly when some vital documents were left merely scattered around the royal apartments, or in open desks, on 10 August. This conclusion leads the authors to three questions which the traditional story of the *armoire de fer* leaves unanswered. (ibid. p.84)

Firstly, why, or under what circumstances, would Louis want to have built so secret a safe, then to use it as he did? Secondly, 'Before carrying them to the Convention, Roland simply could not have had the time to make an inventory, however basic, of this enormous quantity of papers': yet he gave a concise and accurate summary of the papers in his statement on 20 November —did he then read and inventory the contents of the *armoire* before he announced the discovery to the Convention? (cf. Madame Roland's 'furtive opening' [Roland 1821, Vol.2 p.247]). Thirdly, why did Gamain lie about the lock he fitted to the *armoire*? 'He certainly could not have fooled Louis XVI if he built the *armoire* for him: he could have fooled Roland, who knew nothing about locks, but why would he want to do this?'

These questions admit, say the authors, an obvious answer; 'It was not Louis XVI, but Roland who had the *armoire de fer* built by Gamain'. They then proceed to show how and why this happened.

At this point, their work takes on a more conjectural tone. Having based their claims firmly in the sources, they resort to simple psychological projections. For example, we are told that Roland had a petty and enduring hatred of Louis XVI; Heurtier was indebted to Roland for his promotion after 10 August; and Gamain was a corrupt and self-seeking Jacobin only too willing to endear himself to his masters in Paris. As to how the *armoire* was built, the Girault de Coursacs offer only an account of how it might have been built, and how easy it would have been for Roland. 'Safes and secret cupboards were all the rage: Roland would not have had to think very hard to have conceived the plan'. (Girault de Coursac 1982, p.88) Having recruited his accomplices, Roland took measures to ensure that the noise made by Gamain's excavations would not attract attention. Using the excuse that the construction of the new chamber in which the Convention would sit made the Tuileries vulnerable to penetration by counter-revolutionaries, Roland published an order in the *Moniteur* advising that;

> from this evening, 18 September, all entrances to the gar-
> den of the Tuileries Palace will be closed at 9 o'clock. The
> gate from the hall to the garden will be closed permanently.
> (*Moniteur*, No.234)

Gamain then built the *armoire* and was unable to resist the temptation to fit the door with a cheap lock, knowing that Roland would not know the difference between a 'security lock' and an 'ordinary lock'.

On 20 November, Roland was able to take the papers to the Convention as soon as he 'discovered' them, because he had had plenty of time to study them—his office was in the Tuileries Palace, and it would have been easy for him to put aside a selection of papers in the confusion after 10 August. His mistake was to accompany his announcement with an accurate summary of the documents. His political vanity left him open to damaging attacks by the Montagnards, and hastened the end of his political career.

This then is the essence of the case against Roland. The *armoire de fer* was a 'stratagem to dishonour and discredit the King in the eyes of public opinion'. (Girault de Coursac 1982, p.93) It was a small but significant facet of the Jacobin's compounded attack on Louis's public image. Yet how secure is this case? Two assumptions based on the sources quoted above are of fundamental importance—if, by the introduction of new evidence, they can be shown to be false, then the conjectural evidence falls with them. The

first assumption is that Roland must have read the *armoire* papers before
20 November, because his description of them was incompatible with the
time he had to examine them on that date. The second is that Gamain
fitted the *armoire* with a cheaper lock than the 'security lock' he claimed to
have fitted on 1 December; this in order to profit from Roland's ignorance
on the subject of locks, whereas Louis XVI was a keen amateur craftsman.

Roland and the armoire

The Girault de Coursacs omit a vital piece of evidence in their case against
Roland. On the evening of 20 November, having challenged the Minister
in the Convention in the afternoon, Goupilleau made a statement in the
Jacobin Club from which it is possible to reconstruct Roland's movements.
(Aulard 1889-97, Vol.4 p.498) Goupilleau and a colleague, Laloy, both members of the Commission of Twenty-Four, had been working in the Tuileries
from 9.30 a.m. on the morning of the 20th. Roland arrived in the royal
apartments some time after they had begun and Goupilleau was specific
that Roland spoke in the Convention at 12.30 p.m. The journey from the
Tuileries to the Manège where the Convention sat would have taken at most
20 minutes. Because Gamain forced the lock on the door of the *armoire*,
the time taken before the papers were uncovered would have been no more
than 10 or 15 minutes after arriving at the Palace. Thus assuming Roland
did not reach the apartments until 10 o'clock, he still had a clear two hours
in which to examine the papers. Goupilleau asked the Jacobins 'How, given
so little time, could he have analysed' the papers?

Looking again at Roland's description on 20 November, one is struck
not so much by its exactness as by its lack of specific detail. Comparing his
imprecise summary with the details of the official catalogue of the papers,
it becomes clear that his knowledge was compatible only with a cursory
and superficial examination. For example, he described 'a large number of
plans relative to his Guards, his Household, the Armies...' Had he really
been familiar with the documents, he would have known that the number
of 'plans for the Armies' was significantly less than that of the other types.
Furthermore, the bulk of the *armoire* papers were described simply as 'all
sorts of schemes to do with the Revolution', which is hardly indicative of
detailed knowledge.

The question, then, is whether Roland could have compiled the description he gave in roughly two hours. It is highly probable that he could.
As Minister of the Interior, not to mention his experience before the Revolution as an Inspector of Manufactures, he was used to dealing with large
amounts of paperwork, much of which had to be read at speed. Indeed, he

stated this implicitly in the Convention. Defending the delays experienced by a '*décret d'accusation*', Roland said on 20 November:

> I will give an explanation of the steps taken for the execution of this decree tomorrow; as I have more than 700 or 800 letters to read, and as many replies and orders to dispatch, each day, I can't keep all the revelant facts in my memory at once. (*A.P.* Vol.LVII p.601)

Two hours would have been plenty of time for Roland to make an initial survey of the papers—all he really needed was to get the gist of what the *armoire* contained.

There remains Roland's letter of 22 January, where he claimed that he had not even had time to read the papers, but had taken them straight to the Convention. When this letter was read out, the deputy Dartygoeyte took up a familiar theme:

> I notice that when Roland brought the papers discovered at the Tuileries, he stated that he had glanced over them; today, contradicting himself, he claims that he only had time to place them in a briefcase. (*Murmurs*) Remember that he said that members of the Assembly were compromised in these papers? I ask you how he could have known this?

Despite this point, the main charge against Roland remained that he had used the time on 20 November to destroy compromising documents, and it was this charge that his letter was intended to refute, as his last sentence made perfectly clear. 'My swiftness proves that I neither wanted, nor was able, to remove anything'. The letter is a clumsy defence of Roland's political blunder in opening the *armoire* as he did; it is not as damaging as the authors would claim.

Thus, the argument that Roland must have read the *armoire* papers before 20 November, and was therefore implicated in the construction of the safe, appears unconvincing.

Gamain and the armoire

The testimony here is rather more complex. There does appear to be a contradiction between Gamain's statement on 1 December that the *armoire* was closed by a security lock and the evidence in the report of Bolot and Borie. Unfortunately, they only describe the lock as '*une serrure*'. The clue as to the sort of lock that was fitted to the *armoire* comes from their remark that the key was common to three other locks in the royal apartments. According to the Girault de Coursacs, this must mean that the key was a master key which would not be able to open a 'security lock'.

In the eighteenth century, the European lock was nothing
better than a mere bolt, held in place by a spring... The only
impediment to opening it was the wards which the key had to
pass before it could turn in the keyhole... A small collection
of skeleton keys of a few different patterns was all the stock in
trade that a lock-picker required'. (*Encyclopedia Britannica*
13th Edition, London 1926, entry under 'Locks')

The eighteenth century was the century of the warded lock—not until the
1780s with the development in England of the Bramah lock was there a
major technological breakthrough.

While the idea prevailed that a complicated ward gave security, there was room for ingenuity in varying the shape of
the wards.... The locks considered as fastenings had a slender
merit.... they were not very secure. (Tomlinson 1853, p.31-2)

Indeed, the locks shown in the *Encyclopédie des Sciences, des Arts et
des Métiers* as 'locks for cupboards and drawers' are clearly simple warded
locks.

It is unlikely that Gamain fitted the *armoire* with anything but an
'ordinary lock'—Louis would have wanted easy access, and a master key
was the obvious alternative to a large bunch of keys to single locks. Moreover, there was little point in putting an expensive lock on the *armoire*.
Once it was discovered, the *armoire* was essentially useless. Its only *raison
d'etre* was its secrecy, and a 'security lock' would not protect it against a
determined assailant.

There is little doubt that the *armoire de fer* was closed by a standard
lock. Two questions remain: first, why did Gamain testify as he did on 1
December, and second, why did he take the apparently unnecessary step of
forcing the lock on the *armoire* on 20 November when he could easily have
picked it open with a skeleton key?

The answer to the first question lies in the testimony itself. The statement was drafted not by Gamain, who was unfamiliar with the language
of official documents, but by Roland. Thus it was Roland who described
the lock as a 'security lock'; if Gamain queried the description, he would
have been told it was an unimportant detail. For Roland, it was a convenient addition to the image of the *armoire* he intended to reach the public.
Thus Gamain did not lie, nor did he try to cover up his own dishonesty.
He merely did as he was told. This would account too for his action on
20 November. The busy Minister of the Interior would not have been too
concerned about the niceties of picking the lock on the *armoire* when it
could be quickly forced open.

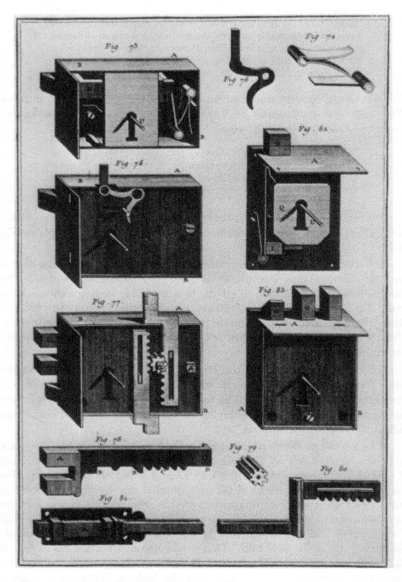

Figure 6. Locks (from the *Encyclopédie)*

A picture of Gamain as a skilled and corrupt actor does not appear convincing. While there is little doubt that he was on the make during the Revolution, it is also clear that he was swimming with the political tide, waiting to see how events would turn out. He did not rush to reveal the *armoire* after 10 August, but waited until the monarchy had been abolished by the Convention, until there was no chance of his revelation backfiring on him.

Gamain's story took a bizarre turn in the eighteen months after November 1792. Perhaps to persuade the Convention to grant him the reward he sought for his service to the Republic, he developed his originally straight-forward testimony. He claimed that on 22 May 1792 Louis XVI had tried to poison him to protect the secret of the newly completed *armoire*. On 17 May 1794, the deputy Peyssard presented a report to the Convention in which Gamain's claim was enthusiastically endorsed. (*A.P.* Vol.XC p.413) A lurid picture was painted of Louis as an habitual assassin who since childhood had been a cruel and treacherous pervert. 'We know how the episodes of the Revolution have been reddened with blood spilt by his homicidal hands'. Although the story of the poisoning is clearly fictitious, it achieved its desired effect. The report portrayed Gamain as a loyal republican, a family man and an innocent victim: he was rewarded a pension of 1200 livres per annum. The Convention was well aware of the propaganda value of the story—it was published in full in the *Moniteur*.

In view of the doubts cast upon the argument presented by the Girault de Coursacs, it seems reasonable to state that Roland did not contract Gamain to build the *armoire de fer*. The basic lack of factual evidence means that although there is no proof either way, it is much more likely that Louis conceived and followed through the idea of a depository for some of his papers. There is no reason to doubt the date given by Gamain in Peyssard's report, and the *armoire*'s construction can confidently be set in May 1792. Louis's motive is clear enough—he wanted a safe and accessible place designed to protect rather than to conceal documents important to the royal cause. It is well documented that at least a week before 10 August, he was taking measures in anticipation of the attack on the Tuileries. For example, he paid off all his debts and settled royal accounts. Louis knew that if the Palace fell, it would be ransacked. It is not unlikely, then, that he destroyed some incriminating papers; but the whole purpose of the *armoire de fer* was to enable him to keep in relative safety documents which he did not want to destroy.

The revolutionaries may have had a field day with the *armoire* documents; but it might be argued that the Convention failed to appreciate that the papers had an ultimately more sinister purpose than that which it attributed to them. As a close examination of the papers will show, here was a coherent royal archive waiting only for a recovery of Louis's power for it to become the official record of the Revolution. When he had the *armoire* built in May 1792, Louis must have thought he might have a long wait.

2. The Armoire as Archive

As we shall see, the revolutionaries themselves never really considered the documents in the *armoire* as a single, constituted body of documents, as an archive of coherent structure. Indeed the whole scenario of recrimination and accusation about the addition or removal of documents that accompanied the discovery effectively militated against such a view. Moreover, even the official publication of the contents only printed less than half the documents (296 out of 726) and added 27 others that were not in the *armoire*. This is further evidence of the same conception of the *armoire* as an essentially random collection to be mined for individual nuggets of evidence. It was this conception that presided over the use of the *armoire* during the King's trial. As for subsequent historians, none has envisaged the collection in any other light and none has sought to analyse it as an archive.

Nonetheless, if we survey the contents of the *armoire de fer* with an eye to a possible organised structure, it becomes clear that we are dealing with a coherent archive. We can base our analysis upon the inventory made by Roland, Carra and Rabaut-Pommier. This inventory was drawn up in the days following the discovery of the *armoire*, and there is every reason to suppose that it reflects the order in which the papers were stored, or at least that no significant regrouping of the papers according to subject matter was undertaken by the three men. This inventory reveals that the papers can be divided into broad groups organised in direct numerical sequence. Our aim here is not so much to attempt an exhaustive analysis of the papers as to provide a general indicative overview of them, and to give, by judicious sampling, something of their range and flavour. By examining the various groups of documents within the archive, it is hoped that we can suggest why Louis might have wanted to keep them.

The documents are not merely the record of a correspondence. They appear to represent a very personal collection of letters and memoirs relating to people and issues important to Louis XVI. As such, they shed light on Louis's attitude to the Revolution and the persistence of his traditional concerns.

The first section (Documents 1 to 91) concerns the problem of the religious settlement during the Revolution. Most of the documents are letters and addresses from members of the clergy to Louis, and many are pleas for help and protection against the religious legislation of 1790 and 1791. They reveal the extent to which the clergy continued to see Louis as the spiritual head of the nation. For example, the Cardinal de Rohan refers to the King as the 'Most Christian King' and the 'Eldest Son of the Church', [Roland cote. 1] and the abbé Rousseau protests that the religious decrees of the National Assembly are a direct challenge to the constitutional principles of the monarchy and the 'true and legitimate authority of the Prince'. These concepts are linked directly with the 'sacred rights of the Church'. [Roland cote. 4]

The documents also reveal something of the pressure the clergy was exerting on Louis to resist the anticlerical bent of the Revolution. Pope Pius VI wrote to him to stress that a political body such as the Assembly had no legitimate powers to interfere with the universal doctrines of the church, and warned Louis that if he approved the Assembly's decrees he risked pushing France into an era of schism and possibly a religious civil war. [Roland cote. 23]

A speech by the Archbishop of Aix, claiming to represent the views of the majority of Bishops in the Assembly, was more helpful. While he recognised that there were clerical abuses to be rooted out, he said that he and his colleagues were concerned that the religious and spiritual interests of the people should be reconciled with the nation's civic and political interests. He suggested the formation of a National Ecclesiastical Council to provide a forum for reconciliation. [Roland cote. 33]

Louis continued to receive letters from the clergy in 1792, particularly from the heads of institutions that faced disruption or closure as the legislation concerning the regular orders began to be applied. For example, on 18 April a letter from the Mother Superior of the Filles de la Charité of Paris asked him to ensure that her establishment was saved from interference, and to refuse his sanction to the decree of 6 April which had suppressed secular congregations. [Roland cote. 33] A typical letter pleaded:

> Sire, a community in tears throws itself at your feet, to im-
> plore the help of your power against the most unjust activities,etc...
> [Roland cote. 44]

It is very likely that this chorus of clerical complaint had an effect on Louis. It is well known that he felt particularly at odds with the Revolution over the religious question, and the *armoire* papers indicate how closely he was kept informed of the effects of the Assembly's legislation on the clergy.

If the correspondence enhanced his belief that he should resist anticlericalism, however, it offered him little help in formulating a workable policy. This is particularly clear in his draft of a letter to the Bishop of Clermont. [Roland cote. 12] This letter has received considerable attention. It was cited during the King's trial, and Jordan has written that the letter can be included among 'those that proved Louis's hatred of the Revolution'. [Jordan 1979, p.73] The draft in the *armoire* is undated, but the reply from Clermont was written on 16 April 1791. [Roland cote. 13] As Louis specifically requests that Clermont reply before noon the day after he receives the letter, Louis must have written on 15 April. It is no coincidence that news of the Papal Bull *'Caritas'* reached Paris that day. The Bull, condemning the Civil Constitution of the Clergy, placed Louis in a difficult position. On the one hand, its firm statement of papal opinion clarified a long-standing issue. On the other hand, it placed the onus of concession on those who were least likely to concede, the revolutionaries, and set the seal on the schism within the church. Not unnaturally, Louis's immediate reaction was to write to a spiritual peer asking for advice on his conduct in Easter week:

> I am writing to you on the subject of my Easter duties. Can
> I, or must I, perform them in the next fortnight? You know
> how unfortunate it would be if I give the appearance of being
> forced into them. I have never hesitated in remaining at one
> with Catholic pastors in my own affairs. I am also firmly
> resolved fully to re-establish the Catholic faith if I recover
> my power.

If Louis clearly leans towards his traditional role, his desire to restore Catholicism is tempered by the knowledge that the recovery of his power is problematical. He seeks a course by which he can satisfy the demands of the Revolution without compromising his 'loyal' subjects, those who were encouraging him to resist the revolutionary impulse and to reassert his authority.

Interpretation of the letter to Clermont, and of other documents in the *armoire*, depends largely on how one interprets Louis's motives and intentions throughout the Revolution. The attitude of the prosecution in 1792 was that he had consistently worked against the Revolution and was guilty of crimes against the nation. Any statement by Louis would be interpreted in the context of 1792. What may have been a genuine belief a year before became dissimulation. This attitude has been very pervasive in the historiography, but it seems to be inherently teleological.

The second section of the *armoire* papers (Documents 92 to 192) consists of a mixture of documents referring to various aspects of the Royal Household, both civil and military. The Household was of intense concern to the Royal Family, which associated elaborate ritual with such attachments to the royal body. The inclusion in the *armoire* of these papers is indicative that Louis was preserving a personal, intimate archive. The documents include lists of employees, accounts for the Households of the Court, lists of the royal jewels, advice as to how the Civil List might be reformed, and plans for the education of the Dauphin. Some of the meticulous accounts date back to 1784, and have clearly been very deliberately kept. The main sources of royal ritual and patronage, the Household and the Civil List had been dismantled or emasculated in 1791. Yet there is enough information in the *armoire* papers for Louis to have restored both to their original forms. At the point in the Revolution when he decided to save such papers, there had already been a significant drain on personnel who knew the detailed workings of the institutions of the monarchy, institutions which, it is clear from the papers, were extremely complex in their organisation of people and resources. The *armoire* archive was a safeguard against any further loss of knowledge.

The third section (Documents 192 to 231) is a series of letters from Laporte, who was the Intendant of the Civil List. Hated by the revolutionaries, he was quickly condemned and executed after the fall of the monarchy. His letters were used extensively during the King's trial, as they indicate various royal policies which, in the context of late 1792, were regarded as counter-revolutionary. In the printed selection of the documents, 30 of the 31 letters signed by Laporte were included.

Several of the letters refer to the liquidation of the King's Household and the reform of the Civil List, with which Laporte was closely involved. They indicate a policy of attempted damage control—Louis's servants would try to secure the best deal they could.

Laporte's letters also contain the references to Mirabeau which exposed his dealings with the Court and ruined his reputation as a virtuous patriot. Thus, for example, on 2 March 1791, Laporte wrote to Louis that 'Mr. Mirabeau wants a secure income for the future...I'm sure that he is the only man who can really be useful to Your Majesty...' [Roland cote. 221] This revelation of Mirabeau as a greedy servant of the crown convinced the Convention that he no longer deserved his place in the Panthéon; his remains were summarily removed and his sculptured memorial shattered.

Particularly interesting are those letters that suggest an active and positive royal policy in response to the Revolution. Laporte forwarded a draft to Louis in February 1791 which discussed various ways in which royal popularity could be increased in an effort to undermine the radical revolutionaries. [Roland cote. 223] The author displayed an awareness of the value of written propaganda and of espionage, and suggested that the King should follow an elaborate plan to sway public opinion in his favour. The plan contains elements which are extremely evocative of events in April (known as the Saint Cloud affair) and indeed of the Flight to Varennes in June. In other letters, Louis was urged to buy support in the Faubourgs, or to subsidise a more forceful royalist press. [Roland cote. 193–4] It is easy to see why such documents were useful to the prosecution in the trial, although there was little evidence that they reflected actual royal policies. Yet even the suggestion that the King was exposed to positive plans and options implies a far more dynamic picture of Louis than the one we are used to seeing.

The bulk of the *armoire* papers (Documents 232 to 612) may be generally categorised as pieces addressing advice or information, mostly connected with revolutionary politics and administration. The range of correspondants was wide, and the documents they presented varied from the complex policy drafts of Lafayette to humble petitions from groups of Parisian workmen. Within this main section, there are several groups of pieces which deserve particular attention.

There is a series of letters from Talon and Sainte-Foy. [Roland cote. 264-75] One significant document is a letter from Sainte-Foy (an agent of the King) to Laporte (who forwarded it to Louis) dated 9 August 1792— proof that Louis continued to use the *armoire* until the day before the fall of the monarchy. In the letter Sainte-Foy advised that Louis should not contemplate taking refuge in the Assembly if the Tuileries Palace was attacked. He recommended Louis to summon a deputation of 200 members of the Assembly and to demand their protection from the militant sections. [Roland cote. 274]

The *armoire* did contain several letters from émigrés, notably Polignac, and Orléans in his earlier capacity as an ambassador to London. [Roland cote. 311–35] The contents are dull, being restricted to professions of loyalty. None of them contains any evidence that Louis was in dishonourable collusion with counter-revolutionary elements.

Lafayette wrote several important briefs to Louis advising on royal policy and outlining the implications for the Crown of certain revolutionary events. [Roland cote. 340-59] He had a conciliatory attitude to the

Revolution and believed that it would establish 'the best possible order of things for the King and the Nation'. [Roland cote. 357] He shared some of the revolutionaries' fascinated faith in the power of a free constitution to create, or restore, social harmony. He advised Louis that the Crown could no longer hope to survive by steering a course through the interests of the various parties. It would be wrecked on the incompatible ground between the remnants of a parasitic aristocracy and the new force of 'the entire Nation'. [Roland cote. 359] Rather, he believed that the way to success lay in faithful adherence to the Constitution, in convincing people that their constitutional rights would be respected with a 'religious faithfulness' [Roland cote 340], in creating moderate spheres of influence in the Assembly, and in freeing the court of its image of intrigue and plotting. It should be noted that Louis was clearly impressed by some of Lafayette's advice. At the foot of one piece he scribbled that he had read it with particular attention: 'I accept it principles and assumptions, despite the exact application of some of them being unclear...' [Roland cote. 357]

Louis was sent a considerable number of documents discussing the Constitution of 1791. [Roland cote. 394-435] Many of them are long discourses on royal policy and contain typically eighteenth-century notions of political theory. Several use the standard image of the King as the pilot of the national vessel which he must steer away from the rocks of popular power. But the tone of advice varies. Lamerville, writing in 1791, was extreme and reactionary—'Monarchical government must be reestablished in all the fullness of royal authority, without any national assemblies...' [Roland cote. 398] Another writer was more realistic and told Louis that royal government was only possible in France through the 'popular means of a legislative body'. [Roland cote. 169]

The documents inevitably vary in the depth and quality of their analysis of the Revolution. While the Archbishop of Aix could lapse into unhelpful philosophical inanities, [Roland cote. 404] the writer of the detailed 'Mémoire sur le Gouvernement' composed an initially insightful, academic treatise. [Roland cote. 397] The style of analysis is similar to that later used by Tocqueville. The author expressed his opinion that while the voice of reason could still be heard in the midst of the factional fighting, there was hope that order could be restored. He believed that the majority of the people wanted a monarchy but that strong steps would have to be taken to retrieve the royal position. The present state of affairs had come about because a minority 'wanted a revolution when the majority of France wanted only reform'. Such clarity was obviously the result of hindsight, however, because when the author came to suggesting present policy he became muddled and long-winded. Moreover, the policy he recommended was little short of a military coup in favour of the monarchy. Louis was told that the Assembly could be cowed into submission only by force, and the author went so far as to write the speech Louis was to give on his day of triumph. It is unlikely that Louis paid the latter half of the document much attention, as he knew that he did not have nearly enough residual loyalty in the army to attempt such a coup. It is possible, however, that he may have thought back rather wistfully to 1789 when a military coup against the Assembly had been a real option.

The remaining groups of papers consist of correspondence from ministers and officials of the revolutionary period. For example, Dumouriez, Cahier de Gerville, de Grave, Servan, Lacoste and Roland wrote to Louis concerning their ministerial functions and their resignations in 1792. [Roland cote. 435-73] D'Angivilliers reported on the administration of the parks, buildings, hunting lands and paupers of Versailles. [Roland cote. 474-512] Chambonas, Duranthon and Narbonne informed Louis of their resignations. [Roland cote. 513-45] There are also identifiable groups of letters from Delessart [Roland cote. 546-56], Bertrand [Roland cote. 557-68], Thévenard, Duportail, La Tour du Pin, La Luzerne [Roland cote. 569-603], and Necker [Roland cote. 604- 12], mostly relating to their functions as ministers.

The final entries in the catalogue refer to a long manuscript containing a detailed history of the principal events of the Revolution after 23 June 1789, plus a volume containing a treatise on the nature of the law. [Roland cote. 613-25] The former appears to be the first volume of a projected work, for it covers only six months, but in considerable detail.

Clearly, then, the correspondence in the *armoire de fer* issued from a wide range of individuals and institutions, each with their own opinions or requests. The diverse documents have one thing in common—they were all addressed, either directly or indirectly, to Louis XVI. Scattered thinly among the various groups of papers, however, is a number of drafts in Louis's own hand. Most of these drafts are not new in the sense that the final documents exist elsewhere and are well known. Thus they are of limited interest. There are, nevertheless, some drafts written in 1791, one referring to the Saint Cloud Affair, and two others to the Constitutional settlement, which are worth examining.

The draft of Louis's speech to the Assembly on 19 April contained much of the final text that was later delivered, but the structure of the speech was substantially altered. Louis initially emphasised the strength of his attachment to the Constitution and the Declaration of Rights, and claimed that, like other citizens, he had the right to his own religious principles. In his final version, while he left in his statement of belief in the Constitution, he deleted the phrase 'I have the same freedoms as all other citizens', perhaps because he felt it might compromise his position as monarch. [Roland cote. 309]

In a draft speech of 11 August 1791, Louis reflected on his escape to Varennes. [Roland cote. 257] He insisted that his objectives had been honourable. He had wanted to flee from his captivity in order to 'know the wishes of the Provinces at first hand, and to stay in an area near the frontier to disconcert the factions'. He had intended to make an appeal to the nation, and complained that the episode of the journey had been manipulated by the Jacobins. The speech was never delivered.

On 13 September, Louis sent an important letter to the Assembly announcing his acceptance of the Constitution. The draft was considerably shorter than the final document, and it appears that Louis made free use of a paper sent to him by Montmorin. [Roland cote. 114] The sentiments expressed in Louis's letter echoed those of the other drafts. Louis reiterated his faith in the Constitutional ideal, and he stated his firm belief that the monarchy had a valid role to play in France. He said that his aim was to isolate himself from the conflict of factional interests in order to discover the true wishes of the Nation. [Roland cote. 410]

Although the drafts reveal nothing drastically new about Louis XVI, they do highlight the degree to which he was seeking a real compromise with the moderate revolutionaries in the months after Varennes. On the strength of such evidence, it does seem that he genuinely believed in the possibility of a workable constitutional settlement.

The correspondence derived almost entirely from the interest groups or classes who would be expected to make literate appeals to the surviving symbol of the old order. A shared assumption is that to appeal to Louis against the Revolution was not to place him in a situation of conflicting interests. Members of the First and Second Estates continued to turn to the Crown to express their grievances. They continued to use the language of the ancien regime. They implied that the Revolution was a temporary nuisance to be accommodated in order that the old system might be restored. The *armoire* papers are vivid testimony to the failure of the nobles and the clergy to adapt to the changes of the revolutionary period. There is also a significant lack of material from members of the Third Estate. There are two possible explanations for this, both potentially important. The first is that the Assembly had succeeded in establishing itself as the natural forum for popular politics, so that Louis was bypassed as a focus of appeal. The second is that Louis did receive a proportional amount of material from the Third Estate, but that he threw almost all of it away, or at least did not think it worth saving in the *armoire*. If the first explanation is true, it says much about revolutionary politics and the extent of the King's alienation from the people. If the latter case is correct, then Louis's selection of documents for the *armoire de fer* is even more relevatory of his mentality than we might have thought. We have no way of knowing which is more accurate.

Nevertheless, this raises the question as to why Louis kept the *armoire* papers and attributed such obvious importance to them. Was he consciously creating a body of connected documents, or did he merely randomly select the papers from the mass of his correspondence?

Two factors suggest that the *armoire* was a planned archive. The first is the common archival feature that groups of letters (for example, those of Laporte) were catalogued by Roland in near reverse date order. This happens when letters are stored with the last received piece placed on top of the relevant pile, or at the front of the relevant file. There is a further clue in the Catalogue—item 384 is described as the 'cover of a file of papers labelled with the King's writing'. This is the only indisputable reference to the existence of files made by Louis (the other is in Madame Roland's memoirs) and it refers to only one file. But it adds to the general impression that the *armoire* documents do possess a coherence not previously acknowledged by historians.

The second factor is the subject matter of the papers. As the description above shows, the *armoire* contained documents relating to many aspects of Louis's rule. While most of the letters could only have a retrospective purpose, there was a core of documents whose advice on present policy represented a formidable summary of the complex and varied issues facing the Crown. The papers included detailed records of the service received by Louis during the Revolution, so that he would know who had been prepared to stand by the monarchy. When the 'official' history of the Revolution is also considered, it seems fair to conclude that the *armoire* was a safe place where Louis could store papers he planned to use at a later date. If the papers proved incriminating to him in the peculiar context of the trial, it was not because the prosecution realised the purpose of the *armoire de fer*. From Louis's point of view, the papers were informative about others in that they recorded attitudes to the monarchy which, in the event of a recovery of royal power, the authors would either regret or endorse.

Figure 7. The Trial of Louis XVI.

3. The Armoire and Politics

i) The Commission of Twelve

After Roland's anouncement of the discovery of the *armoire*, the Convention ordered a thorough examination of the documents. Initially they would be catalogued by Roland and two secretaries of the Convention, but the bulk of the work would be done by twelve selected deputies whose brief was far wider than that given to Roland. The commissioners were to prepare documents for use in the trial of the King, and to report on any individuals who might be compromised in the papers.

Roland's catalogue was made at the same time as the Commission was starting its work, so it is hard to tell how the papers were classified; but it seems likely that the original order was preserved. The Commission later made a quite separate classification, but always deferred to Roland's in order to authenticate a reference.

The members of the Commission came from differing political backgrounds. The majority was centrist, there were two Girondins and two Montagnards, as well as the anarchist Cloots.

They might be represented as follows:

Centrists: Boussion, Saurine, Bernard, Bolot, Gardien, Rabaut-Pommier

Girondins: Doublet, Lefranc, Pellissier

Montagnards: Borie, Ruamps, Cloots, Ruhl.

Ruhl was ill for the first few days of the Commission's work, and although he later became an important spokesman, he was replaced temporarily by Doublet.

It is possible to follow the aims and progress of the Commission in the reports it made to the Convention. (*A.P.* Vols.LIII - LVI) At the outset, it was hoped that the papers would provide evidence of Louis's betrayal of the nation. When this proved not to be the case, the papers were used against lesser figures. By taking Louis's guilt for granted, the Commission could then claim to be performing the essential task of weeding out traitors and accomplices of the monarchy.

On 22 November, Rabaut-Pommier announced that a preliminary reading of the papers had convinced the Commission of the need to arrest Dufresne-Saint-Léon, *commissaire liquidateur* of the ex-King's Household. His papers and effects should be sealed off pending further investigation. (*A.P.* Vol.LIII p.544)

The following day, Gardien told the deputies that the Commission had found 'a large number of exhibits against the traitor Louis XVI'. He read out a letter from Louis to Bouillé, dated 18 November 1790, concerning the massacre at Nancy. He also read Bouillé's reply. The Commission was then asked to prepare a report on all the papers it judged the most important. Not everyone was impressed by the letters quoted by Gardien - Marat was scathing about these 'letters mentioned by all the newspapers at the time', and he said it was absurd to see Gardien trying to 'give new life to these old crimes by announcing them as a discovery and making them the latest turpitude of the dethroned King'. (*Journal de la Republique* No.56)

On 3 December, Ruhl presented the first of three major reports. His stated concern was to draw attention to documents in which members of the Convention, and ex-deputies of the National and Legislative Assemblies, were implicated. He said some were implicated 'by name, others collectively, and others more vaguely'. Using selected documents, Ruhl named the following: Kersaint, Clavière, Leflos, Dietrich, Dumouriez, Rouyer, Lacoste, Merlin de Thionville, Auger and the current President of the Convention, Barère.

These specific nominations proved less contentious than two documents which made general reference to the Assembly. The first was dated 2 January 1792. Sent to Louis by Talon and Sainte-Foy, it said that

> sixteen of the most powerful members of the Assembly have formed an inviolable coalition. Their support is being bought for three months, and thereafter for as long as the Legislative Assembly lasts.

The second was a letter from Talon to Louis dated 27 July 1792 in which he urged Louis to recruit 'from a number of deputies who have offered themselves for this sort of service'. Such vague remarks gave scope for subjective judgements as to the identity of the 'most powerful of the deputies'.

No sooner had Ruhl finished his report than Barère rose from the President's chair to clear himself from suspicion. In order to speak, he vacated the chair in favour of Guadet. There was an immediate intervention from Cháles, who insisted that Guadet too should give up the chair:

> I ask you whether Guadet wasn't one of the most distinguished members of the last Legislative Assembly. (*Violent murmurs on the Right: some applause from the Tribunes*) Moreover, all those who showed similar patriotism in the Legislative Assembly must be under suspicion.

This intervention threatened to distract the Convention from the original subject of debate. It took a proposal by Rewbell to restore order—the Commission should continue its report, after which Barère could be the first to defend himself. This was adopted by the deputies.

Ruamps then read out a confession which Sainte-Foy had written after his interrogation to justify his conduct, and Borie added a letter of 9 August 1792 which he claimed proved that Sainte-Foy was actively advising Louis XVI. Then Barère rose to speak. His defence was long, detailed and very successful. He was able to resume his presidency immediately. It is worth noting that his facility with dates and quotations leaves no doubt that his defence had been planned in advance. He was either a remarkably astute politician, or, more likely, he had been warned by one of the Commissioners of the precise nature of the document in which his name was mentioned so that he could prepare a rebuttal.

The session continued. Rabaut-Pommier read out the minutes of the interrogations of Sainte-Foy and Saint-Léon. When he had finished, the Convention decreed that 'there are grounds for prosecution against Sainte-Foy, Talon and Saint-Léon'.

Ruhl's second report was presented two days later. The Convention had decreed that it would judge Louis XVI in December, and this was seen as a signal to the Commission to prepare for the trial. Ruhl said that he would 'show the Assembly documents that would paint a picture of the terrible fate being prepared for it by the tyrant and his accomplices'. The Commission could declare an intention, yet it remained bound by the actual nature of the papers. Thus, Ruhl and his colleagues were forced to concentrate more on Louis's 'accomplices' than on the 'tyrant' himself. It is hard in fact to distinguish between the theme of the documents cited on

3 December and those cited on 5 December. In his second report Ruhl was able to damage Louis specifically by reading his letter to the Bishop of Clermont, but the real result of the report was the issuing of warrants for the arrest of seven more suspects, and the ruin of the reputation of Mirabeau. Among thc·e whose arrests were ordered were the royalist journalist, Rivarol; the ex-deputy from the Legislative Assembly, Duquesnoy; and the émigrés d'André and Talleyrand, both of whom had finally fled France in 1792. The Convention also decreed that all the 'documents concerning Louis XVI' would be printed.

It might be suggested that the *armoire* papers were a source of considerable frustration to the Convention, for they failed to provide the concrete proofs initially expected of them. The commissioners had to resort to guilt by association—merely to be mentioned in the papers was grounds for suspicion. Louis's claim at his trial that the bulk of the archive consisted of unsolicited advice, and that his own drafts were nothing more than drafts and not statements of intent or policy, was a shrewd defence because it emphasised the rather innocuous nature of many of the papers.

Ruhl gave his third report on 7 December. (*A.P.* Vol.LIV pp.406-10) His subject here was quite specific —to present papers relating to Dumouriez, the general whose loyalties were under suspicion. The papers fell into two categories, those 'relative to supplies for the army', and those 'which effect him personally'. The documents produced for the first area were so nebulous that some of the deputies lost patience and shouted 'This is all a waste of time!'. Ruhl went on to the second area, and it quickly became clear that the real purpose of the report was to distance Dumouriez from Louis and his agents. A possible reason for this is that the Jacobins wanted to imply that any credit for the turning tide of the war was owed to themselves and not to Louis. Hence the significance of the letters cited below which emphasise a split between Dumouriez and the King over military matters. This is particularly interesting as it appears that the temptation to label Dumouriez as a Girondin ally of the Crown was not as great as the need to claim credit for the victories which had saved France from defeat in war.

Ruhl read out a letter from Laporte to Louis which said, among other things:

> Dumouriez is a revolutionary. I don't think I will ever trust
> him in matters concerning Your Majesty's interests where we
> disagree, nor in negotiations to be held with the Assembly.
> (Rol. cote. 216)

These remarks were greeted by the deputies with applause. The next document read by Ruhl caused a momentary stir—a letter from Dumouriez began with the words 'Your Majesty is the most honest man in his kingdom': but the letter was a complaint about Louis's military appointments and Dumouriez had written nothing seriously incriminating. (Rol. cote. 217) A further document produced more applause—Sainte-Foy wrote to Louis on 14 June 1792 with the news that Dumouriez had not followed 'any of my advice to the letter'. (Rol. cote. 275)

Ruhl's three reports made up the main work of the Commission of Twelve. On 6 December, the Convention had created a new Commission of Twenty-One, which included all the members of the Twelve. Its task was to prepare the exhibits for Louis's trial, and the focus of attention shifted away from the *armoire de fer* towards a wider corpus of documents. There were, however, several follow-up reports on the arrest warrants issued as a result of Ruhl's evidence.

In three appearances between 31 December and 7 January, Boussion successfully proposed the dropping of charges against Drucourt, Duquesnoy and d'André. The reason in each case was lack of evidence.

On 12 January, Thuriot proposed a decree transferring to the Criminal Court of Paris the cases of those ex-deputies still under arrest in the capital. Following interrogation, they would be sent home under guard. This was adopted. (*A.P.* Vol. LVII p.4)

On 22 January, Gardien presented a major report. Following the execution of the King on the previous day, the Commission might have relaxed, its main responsibility over. However, it appears that the impetus to weed out traitors associated with the crown remained strong. It might be suggested that such concerns were a useful distraction from economic problems or political uncertainty. Or it may have been that the Commission had uncovered a case of what was believed to be genuine corruption, and was determined not to let the matter die. Gardien claimed that five men had conspired together to 'ensure by corruption that the selling off of the accounts and pensions attached to the former King's Household was successful'. He named the five as Sainte-Foy, Delessart, Saint-Léon, Laporte and Demarivaux, and cited documents to support his case. Gardien then said that the Commission had gone on to investigate rumours of corruption against members of the Committee which had been responsible for the settlement of Louis's affairs under the Constitution of 1791. Suspicion had fallen in particular on those who had voted for the Civil List put forward by Saint-Léon, as this List was seen to be favourable to the King. After cross-examining the Committee members, the Commission had concluded that there was proof of corruption against five of them, that two were open to suspicion, and the remaining five were innocent. The Convention decreed a further interrogation of the twelve men, and asked for a delay in proceedings. (*A.P.* Vol.LVII p.543-547)

On 4 February, Gardien submitted a new decree concerning the men he had named on 22 January. Hardly had the debate begun, when Dartygoeyte made an important speech which effectively finished the investigative work of the Commission of Twelve. He made three points about Gardien's speech of the 22nd. Firstly, he said that despite Gardien's admission under questioning that positive proof of corruption existed against only two of the 17 men he had mentioned, 11 of them had béen imprisoned or under guard for over six weeks, without any charges being brought. Secondly, the Commission had made an arbitrary and legally inadequate distinction between those members of the Committee who had voted for the Civil List for corrupt reasons and those who had merely approved it. Thirdly, he claimed, it was unreasonable to send ex-deputies in front of the Criminal Court on charges of treason when there were no proofs against them. Dartygoeyte appealed to the Convention to recognise that the Commission had tried to read too much into the documents on which the case was based. It had attributed motives of conspiracy where there may have been only ignorance. He proposed that only Demarivaux and the Committee member, Amy, should remain under investigation as there did seem to be solid evidence against them. The rest of the suspects should be set free.

By agreeing with Dartygoeyte, the Convention signalled to the Commission that its essential work was done. Louis XVI had been executed, and the guilt of several of his close associates had been confirmed by the documents found in the *armoire de fer*, associates both dead (for example, Mirabeau and Laporte) and living (for example, Sainte-Foy and Saint-Léon). It had taken a full two months after the nature of the papers had become clear for the Convention to admit that the context in which the documents were originally written could be important in deciding the motive of the correspondent, and even then this admission only applied to a number of ex-deputies who had merely been mentioned in the papers.

As if to emphasise the passing of the Commission of Twelve, Borie successfully proposed the release of Parent de Chassy, who had been under arrest since 5 December 1792. Speaking on 7 March 1793 he said that 'No statement in the documents casts any slur upon his probity'. (*A.P.* Vol.LIX p.680)

ii) Girondins and Montagnards

On 20 September 1792, the Convention had opened in an atmosphere of harmony which owed much, according to the deputy Levasseur, to the innocence of the newly elected members. Following the overthrow of the monarchy, they were initially preoccupied with the radical business of establishing the Republic. From his later viewpoint, Levasseur was amazed at the naivety of the bulk of uncommitted deputies as they followed the example of the radicals in the Legislative Assembly and crowded on to the benches of the Left. He found it hard to date the formation of divisions within the Convention and thus fell back on the teleological idea that the deputies themselves were unaware of the existence of two 'parties'. In fact, it is clear that like the National Assembly before it, the Convention accepted the role of primary agent of national regeneration, but could reach no consensus as to how regeneration was to be achieved. The deputies agreed that the monarchy must be abolished in favour of a Republic, but the nature of that Republic remained controversial. To some extent it might appear facile to say that the splits that emerged between rival groups of deputies were caused primarily by the advocacy of competing visions of the course of the Revolution. However, it is important to remember that in the period after 10 August, the ability to direct that course was literally at stake in a way that it had never been before then. Although, as we shall see later on, Louis XVI remained a potent political symbol, he had no chance of regaining his power; the removal of his influence, however small and secondary this may have been, was a vital factor shaping politics at this point.

Yet the harmony described by Levasseur lasted no longer than a few days. It quickly became clear that 'the Convention could hardly have been more than a battleground for forces already aligned by earlier events'. (Sydenham 1969, p. 127) The nature of these forces, and the issues over which they fought, are well known, and need detain us only briefly here.

Perhaps the central political problem facing the Convention was its relationship with the city of Paris, and the Commune in particular. Parisian radicalism had gained a not inconsiderable voice in the legislature—for example, the elections for the city had been held in the Jacobin Club, and among those elected by the capital were Danton, Robespierre and Marat. Deputies who had been elected by the provincial assemblies soon began to fear the influence of these men among the Paris mob. Moderates grew increasingly suspicious that the radicals might mobilise the sections to overthrow the Convention. A vocal group of deputies from the Gironde including Vergniaud, Gensonné and Guadet joined other men like Brissot and Roland to form a loose association defined more by a shared opposition to radical policies than by any coherent political allegiance. This grouping, generally known as the 'Girondins', accused the more radical deputies, the 'Montagnards', of collusion in the September Massacres, of being sympathetic to extreme radical attitudes and of favouring Paris against the rest of France. The Montagnards in turn accused the Girondins of corruption, personal ambition, military ineptitude and reactionary economic policies.

General tensions were exacerbated by personal rivalries between prominent members of these two bodies of opinion. For example, Brissot and Robespierre fought a long battle for control of the Jacobin Club, a conflict which ended in defeat for Brissot who suffered expulsion on 10 October. By then, the Convention itself was established as the stage on which the principal issues would be fought, although the Jacobin Club remained an important testing ground for Montagnard cohesion before official debates. Thus, well before Roland's discovery of the *armoire de fer* in November, serious divisions had emerged in the Convention. These divisions were initially to determine the reception of the documents which Roland uncautiously uncovered. As events unfolded, however, it became apparent that the *armoire de fer* was to have a much more potent impact.

Within this broad context of Girondin–Montagnard rivalry, the specific context in which Roland brought the *armoire* papers to the Convention was crucial. Debate on the fate of Louis XVI had begun on 13 November, but throughout the pre-trial period the Girondins were divided among themselves and advocated no common policy. This left them open to accusations from the Montagnards that they wanted to avoid decisions which might lead to Louis's death; it was widely accepted that if the King came to trial he would be found guilty and much of the political manoeuvering at this point was looking further ahead to Louis's possible punishment. In contrast to Girondin uncertainty and lack of cohesion, the Montagnards presented a powerful case in favour of either summary execution or immediate opening of trial proceedings.

Debate on the deposed monarch's fate took place against a background of inconclusive committee work. The Legislative Committee under the lawyer Mailhe had asserted that Louis could be tried by the Convention; but the Committee of Twenty-Four, headed by the Girondin Valazé, had failed to provide the evidence needed for a prosecution, despite reporting twice to the Convention on 4 October and 6 November. This latter report had embarrassed the Girondin leadership, which was then put under further pressure by Montagnard calls for Louis's immediate execution. Because it was discovered by one of their leaders, the *armoire de fer* was potentially political manna for the Girondins—carefully used it was the most coherent body of royal papers in existence, and would prove that accusations that they favoured Louis XVI were false.

We have already seen, however, that Roland blundered. His careless opening of the *armoire* provided the Montagnards with the opportunity to attack not just him, but also his Girondin allies. His crime was to have destroyed vital evidence that would have revealed Girondin complicity with royal treason. Camille Desmoulins formulated this accusation unambiguously. There was no need, he proclaimed, for documentary proof of Roland's alliance with the former nobility:

> What!! Roland, on his own, for we cannot count his two Brissotin accomplices, dared secretly to remove from the state's archives evidence of a four-year conspiracy! He dared to open the *armoire de fer* on his own, when most of the Convention knows that he must have removed from it damning evidence against himself. It is well known that his friends Guadet, Vergniaud and Gensonné did a deal with the King on 9 August, but evidence of this was not found among the papers. It is a remarkable feature of this story of counter-revolutionary intrigue that vital evidence is missing at every point where the Brissotins are accused of betraying us to the Court... (Desmoulins 1793, p.56)

The attack on Roland, inside and outside the Convention, developed rapidly along these lines. The Montagnards' initial offensive gives a good indication of the suspicion that existed between the two groups. While the detailed contents of the *armoire* were not known, the fear that the Girondins might use the documents for factional purposes is evident. Already on 20 November, Basire and Robespierre spoke to this effect in the Jacobin club. Basire was sure that the papers would be found to contain evidence 'not against Brissot and his faction, but against true Jacobins', while Robespierre echoed that 'not only could Roland have removed documents, he could also have added them'. (Aulard 1889-97, vol.IV p.498)

Three days later, Marat reiterated this argument by pointing out that Roland had failed to call a meeting of the Committee of General Security which had been elected on 17 October. Marat drew elaborate word pictures of the imprisoned Louis XVI ordering Roland to suppress documents found in the *armoire*, and of Roland seizing the opportunity to insert new ones. He added sarcastically that Roland had been accompanied only by 'two of his cronies'. This point led him to the general conclusion that no court could accept any accusations based on these papers, unless they were properly authenticated (signed, for example) or else referred to some 'known enemy of the Revolution'. With a final Parthian shot he asserted that 'Roland is known to be the head of the Brissotin clique, rumoured to be full of accomplices of Louis Capet'. (*Journal* no.54)

Once the content of the papers was known, the attack hardened. An argument originally designed to protect Montagnards became an excellent offensive weapon. Marat could be much more dismissive and brutal on 25 November:

> No sane man will believe that you found anything in that hole
> in the wall except what you put there yourself; you obviously
> removed vital evidence, notably the copy of the Treaty of
> Pilnitz signed by Louis XVI. (*Journal* no.56)

The same day, the Section des Piques announced that Roland had lost its confidence and the General Council of the Commune set up a Committee to examine his conduct. (*Moniteur* no.330) Both actions reflect the Girondin–Montagnard split, and indicate the extent to which the Girondin leaders were alienated from the radicals in Paris. The Montagnards enjoyed the support of a vocal power group outside the Convention which was able, because of its proximity, directly to influence the political atmosphere. Roland publicly spoke out against what he and his allies saw as the undesirable dominance by Paris of the nation, but the Girondins were appealing to a far less cohesive and accessible audience.

Proceedings in the Convention during December and January record Roland's eclipse amidst increasing fratricidal tension. On several occasions he was almost arbitrarily singled out for abuse. Thus, for instance, on 16 December, when Merlin de Thionville denounced the divisions among deputies as inhibiting the passage to a successful Republic and talked of banning the Bourbon dynasty, Duhem leapt in to accuse Roland of being the principal cause of division and to demand his expulsion from the Ministry. (*A.P.* Vol.LV p.84) On 3rd January, the discovery of papers at the house of Thierry, Louis's valet, allowed Robespierre to have a field day with a demand that Roland should not be allowed to remove them. When Roland picked up the insult, Robespierre indulged in a series of amusing innuendoes. (*A.P.* Vol.LVI p.169-70, p.180)

It is clear that the attack mounted against Roland over the *armoire de fer* was in large part based on sophistry. It was based on the unsubstantiated assertion that Roland and his friends were allies of the monarchy. It was based on the proposition that because papers that his accusers deemed should have been there were not, then they had been removed by Roland— even though there was no evidence that they had ever existed.

Roland's handling of the *armoire de fer* was a grave political mistake because it laid him open to precisely the sort of accusations cited above. Not only did he have no adequate defence against even the wildest conjectures, his behaviour at the moment of the discovery of the *armoire* served to accredit those assertions and propositions that formed the basis of the Montagnard attack on the Girondins. At root, Roland could only identify the accusations against him for what they were— 'gratuitous and untrue smears'. (*A.P.* Vol.LVI p.180) But his own conduct had robbed this defence of conviction. In the complex political context set out above, it was a peculiarly damaging position to be in.

Roland's defence did not change between his statement on 21 November and his letter of resignation written on 22 January. In the letter, he recognised that the attention he had received over the *armoire de fer* was largely his own fault, and that 'lacking any other way of incriminating me', his opponents had concentrated on this episode and damaged his credibility beyond repair. (*A.P.* Vol.LVII p.601)

There can be no doubt that Roland's resignation was finally prompted by Danton's eulogy of the assassinated deputy, Lepeletier Saint-Fargeau, on 21 January. Danton made an emotional appeal for unity and repeated Duhem's charge that Roland's presence in government was divisive. He demanded that 'for the good of the Republic, Roland should no longer be a minister'. (Morse Stephens 1892, vol.2 p.184-5) It was with some relief that the Convention accepted the proffered resignation on 23 January.

The *armoire de fer* affair, therefore, was instrumental in discrediting Roland and bringing about his eventual fall from power. More important, however, in the context of the factional struggle of the winter 1792–3, was its role in giving apparent solidity to general Montagnard accusations about the Girondins' political probity. Ultimately, it was the growing acceptance of the truth of these accusations by people inside and outside the Convention that was fundamental to the decline of Girondin credibility.

iii) Reality and imagery

In the light of the standard historiography, the most extraordinary aspect of the *armoire de fer* is how little use of it was actually made during the King's trial. Although it appeared to be a major source of evidence (and some elements were exploited) it was kept very much in the background during the King's appearances in the Convention. In fact, the only direct reference to it came on 11 December when Louis was being shown the papers upon which the charges against him were based:

> Valazé: Several unsigned documents found in the Tuileries in the secret opening in the palace walls—they refer to the spending of money in order to win popularity.
> The President: Before you answer this charge, I would like you to answer a preliminary question: did you have built a cupboard with an iron door in the Tuileries?
> Louis: I know nothing of this. (*Moniteur* no.349)

This reference was made even more obscure by the fact that the documents which Valazé went on to cite (and which he implied had been found in the *armoire de fer*) were not catalogued by the Commission of Twelve,

but by the Commission of Twenty-Four and the Committee of General
Security. This meant that they had not been found in the *armoire* but
had been gathered from a wide range of sources. Moreover, they pertained
to particularly damaging accusations that Louis had been trying to buy
support in the suburbs of Paris, and that he had been connected with the
army of the émigré princes through his own personal bodyguard. (*A.P.*Vol.
LV p.12)

It is not impossible that the obscurity of Valazé's reference to the
armoire was part of a cover-up to protect Roland from embarrassing inves-
tigations of the *armoire*. There are, however, other explanations. It suited
the prosecution to blur their case at the edges, for this allowed them to link
the most damaging symbols of royal guilt with the most damaging documents: whether this was a valid connection was to remain unquestioned.
This achieved an important effect. Not only did the mystery of the *armoire de fer* survive the trial intact, but it was actually enhanced by the
suggestion that the *armoire* was the source of all the proofs of Louis's guilt.

It might also be argued that the reason for Valazé's opacity lay not
so much in the Girondin–Montagnard struggle over Roland as in the wider
and more significant struggle over the King's trial. The *armoire* was far
more potentially embarrassing to Louis XVI than it was to Roland.

The selectivity of the Convention's attitude to the *armoire*'s contents
was already visible in the official publication which began to appear from
December 1792. A similar approach underlay the composition of the trial
documents that formed the prosecution's brief. Thirty-nine *armoire* documents were specified in the trial. This compares with 26 denunciations of
Louis and his associates made to the police, and 35 letters from separate
sources of which Louis could have had no knowledge. (*A.P.* Vol.LV p.519–
23) While the *armoire* papers were clearly important, then, the prosecution
paid little attention to the possible relation of the documents to one another. This might be explained by their certainty that Louis was guilty
and that the *armoire* proved their case. However, that scarcely explains
why such half-hearted use was made of what should have constituted the
major body of evidence. It is more likely that the prosecution in fact had
no sense of the *armoire*'s coherence as an archive. Certain items could be
singled out, and could have considerable effect—for example, Louis's letter to Clermont. But these documents had only individual impact and it
is impossible to assess whether this was any greater than, say, the police
evidence.

If one accepts that the *armoire* was merely one of several important
sources of evidence during the trial, then the question remains as to how
it acquired its reputation (implicit, for example in the histories quoted at

the beginning of this book) as the source of the vital proofs against Louis XVI. The answer lies in an examination of the way in which the *armoire* was portrayed by the revolutionaries and in an analysis of the nature of the trial itself.

Before the revolutionary period, 'the importance of mystery to the integrity of monarchic rule... cannot be overstressed'. (Walzer 1974, p.5) The concept of mystery was supported both by the supernatural qualities owned by the royal body as God's deputy on earth, and by the institution-alised ritual which presented the monarchy to the people as an image whilst simultaneously removing it from reality. The traditional conception of the monarchy was reiterated by Louis XV to a recalcitrant Paris Parlement at the so-called '*Séance de la Flagellation*' in 1766:

> As if anyone could forget that there resides in my person alone
> the sovereign power of which the natural characteristics are
> the spirit of consultation, justice and reason; ... that public
> order in its entirety emanates from me, and that the rights
> and interests of the nation, which some dare to regard as
> a separate body from the monarch, are necessarily united
> with my rights and interests and repose only in my hands.
> (Rothney 1969, p.177)

This was a total denial of the Parlement's claim to constitute a single and indivisible body representing the nation—this function belonged only to the crown. Yet as early as the 1750s there began to develop in France a new political culture that challenged these traditional conceptions. In 1753, Gilbert de Voisins wrote:

> Today the very foundations of the constitution and the order
> of the state are placed in question. The different degrees of
> authority and power, the rules and measures of obedience,
> the mysteries of the state are indiscreetly debated under the
> eyes of the vulgar. (Baker 1982, p.213)

To a large extent this movement was caused by the extension of royal government in response to the problems of the eighteenth century. In extending its public authority, the monarchy necessarily depersonalised royal power, and political authority in general.

As the functions of the state came to be demystified, so the monarchy came under closer scrutiny. The King was still nominally absolute in 1789, but 'he could no longer act out the ideology that made absolutism credible'. (Walzer 1974, p.26) The cause of revolution lay partly in the failure of the political language used in 1766 by Louis XV. For Tocqueville, while the King continued to use the language of absolutism, 'in reality he constantly obeyed a public opinion, which he consulted, feared and flattered unceasingly'. (Tocqueville 1956, Bk.2 Ch.4)

A key purpose of the trial was to deny the ideology and mystique of the monarchy by destroying the personal inviolability of the King. This was achieved essentially by declaring that Louis was no longer a King, but a citizen who was guilty of a specific crime against the nation. The nation was thereby given a conceptual identity and will which was distinct from Louis's actions.

Louis's trial juxtaposed the institution and the person of the monarchy in a peculiarly effective way. On the one hand, the Jacobins portrayed an ancien-regime, absolute monarchy and attributed to it a set of characteristics. As well as being counter-revolutionary, secretive, furtive, power-seeking and retributive, it was corrupt and anti-egalitarian. On the other hand, there was the potent image of Louis XVI, bowed but not broken by the events of 10 August, and able to retain his personal dignity through the period of his captivity and trial. One of the problems faced by the Jacobins was how convincingly to link these separate images, without arousing sympathy for the King. This can be seen clearly in the care taken by the Convention to avoid heckling Louis during his appearances there.

The importance of the *armoire de fer* was that it provided a real link between two apparently contradictory conceptions. It suited the Jacobins that the link could be made without paying too much attention to what the *armoire* actually contained. Indeed, if it had been shown that the *armoire* was a systematic archive, this would have set up a coherent model of royal authority, a model which would have been in stark opposition to the existing portrayal of the monarchy. As it stood, the monarchy could not challenge the revolutionary claim to articulate the General Will, but seen in a different, purposeful light it could seriously undermine that claim. However, the *armoire de fer*, by being private, secret and concealed, was contrary to the model of universality, trust and transparency implied in a culture of royal authority that depended on display and ritual. Instead of providing 'consultation, justice and reason' it could be presented as contingent, arbitrary and individual. That it existed proved that Louis had breached the code of honour through which absolute monarchy was justified. That it contained potentially subversive material broke down the identification between King and Commonweal. By exploitation of popular beliefs about the nature of kingship, the private figure of the deposed monarch could be made to appear a profound political danger.

From the moment of its discovery the *armoire de fer* was a powerful source of imagery. Its secret nature was compounded by the mysterious behaviour of Roland, who announced that the *armoire* was important not because of its contents which he had not yet read, but because of the obvious care with which it had been concealed. Marat, similarly ignorant, immediately suggested that the *armoire* must have contained the jewels which rumour had always accused the monarchy of possessing. Although Marat's suggestion was ridiculed by Roland on 21 November, its symbolic connotations gave it a significance in the popular consciousness far greater that its factual inaccuracy deserved. The connection between jewels and the monarchy was obvious on several levels, from the sacred attributes of kingship like the crown and the sceptre, to more sordid episodes like the Diamond Necklace Affair.

The Jacobins were always able to make effective propaganda by evoking images that had ready association in the popular mind. It was extremely difficult for the monarchy to contain the revolutionary discourse because it lacked the positive drive to oppose the essentially negative, destructive accusations of the radicals.

The best example of the use of propaganda to convey a particular image of the *armoire de fer* is a print which was widely circulated at the time of Louis's trial. The print depicts the opening of the *armoire*. Gamain, wearing the revolutionary cockade, has just forced open the doors using his locksmith's tools. Roland, seated, looks on in horror and amazement at what issues forth—a stream of letters, documents and large bound volumes bursts out. A huge drape decorated with fleurs-de-lys has been moved aside to reveal the large cupboard. Inside a full-size but skeletal Mirabeau sits unhappily on the pile of books. With one hand he reaches for Louis XVI's fallen crown: in the other he holds a small bag of money. Above the *armoire* hangs an oval picture which depicts a serpent with the head of Louis spewing into a cap which bears the revolutionary cockade.

The artist clearly implies that in order to reveal the corrupting effect of monarchy, several layers have had to be stripped off. The moving aside of the drape symbolises the victory of the Republic over the monarchy; but the fortified doors have to be broken down before the royal demise is uncovered, laid bare for all to see. As the secret royal papers tumble out from behind the locked doors, the King's defeat is represented both by Mirabeau's reduced presence and by the fallen crown which he is still trying to rescue. The bag of money in Mirabeau's right hand, held rather defiantly, symbolises betrayal, and this theme is emphasised by the oval picture. The picture, which has also been hidden from view, shows Louis as a serpent pouring vomit on to the Revolution, symbolised by the cap (worn also by Gamain who is the embodiment of the Republic in the main picture). The moderate Roland is aghast at the monster Gamain has uncovered. It is the proverbial skeleton in the cupboard.

The print reveals the essential nature of the Jacobin discourse during the trial. In order to destroy the mystique of the monarch, Louis's opponents found that they had to emphasise the mystery and secrecy of the institution. In order to break down the apparent contrast between Louis and his office, they made use of symbols to place their connection beyond doubt. These symbols appealed to an absolute monarchy which had already been overthrown. If a seemingly genuine link could be made, whether by use of evidence or propaganda, between this discredited institution and the fallen Louis XVI, then the outcome of the trial would be a formality.

Discovered at a time when the fall of the monarchy was an irreversible fact, the *armoire de fer* was at once proof of the justice of that fall, and a symbolic and forceful reminder of what had been overthrown. The image of a secret cache of documents concealed in an iron cupboard was used by the Jacobins to re-emphasise the extent to which Louis was living in the past, believing that he continued to reign after he had ceased to rule. Although it was little mentioned in proceedings, the *armoire* set the context of the trial of Louis XVI, not only in the sense that it provided some of the evidence with which he could be convicted, but also by presenting the people with a clear focal point for their previously diffuse image of royal treachery. However, it was the existence of the *armoire*, together with what it implied about Louis (and, by extension, the monarchy) that was more important than what the contents of the *armoire* actually were and what the *armoire* actually revealed about Louis. Indeed, a study of the *armoire* as archive or as legal evidence would have been inimical to its symbolic importance.

DOCUMENTS

A selection of documents from the *armoire de fer* was published following the work of the Commission of Twelve, as outlined in Chapter 2. This selection was reprinted in the *Archives parlementaires*, the massive collection of transcripts of the Revolutionary assemblies which in some ways is comparable with Hansard. Historians have tended to utilise the documents available in the *Archives parlementaires* without having recourse to the originals. This is fraught with dangers: partly because the accuracy and reliability of the *Archives parlementaires* are not above reproach, partly because the Commission of Twelve had a clear purpose in mind, so that many of the documents it published were designed to provide evidence of Louis XVI's anti-revolutionary behaviour.

The present collection of documents from the *armoire de fer* has been trawled from the manuscripts themselves. These are now largely housed in the Archives Nationales in Paris, Series C 183–7, where they are bound in the volumes created by the Commission of Twelve. Some of the key documents, notably those written by Louis himself and extracted for his trial, are located in separate cartons which cover the King's prosecution. Several documents are on display in the Musée de France, housed in the same building as the Archives. Many of them appear in print for the first time, and the vast majority have never been previously available in English translation. They are listed in what is—as far as it is possible to judge—roughly chronological order, and the catalogue number given them by Roland is noted. Brief notes have been provided to help to set individual documents against their political context. These have been kept to a minimum, however, so as to let the documents speak for themselves wherever possible.

The selection provided here represents only a small fraction of the archive as a whole. However, my aim has been to avoid merely mining the documents for nuggets which may prove a particular case or argument, and rather to try to give a representative cross-section of the types of document which were found in the *armoire de fer*.

Extracts from an anonymous memorandum entitled 'Account of the Princi-
pal Events of the Revolution and the Decrees of the National Assembly; their
agreements and differences with the Cahiers of the Bailliages, the plans pre-
sented to the First Assembly of Notables, and the King's Declaration of 23
June '89.' (Roland cote.613)

The Tennis Court Oath and the King's Declaration.

Based on the balance of powers, the Estates General ceased to exist when a
single chamber had the audacity to usurp them all. Mr. Necker reaped the
harvest of his contemptuous attitude to the people. The throne tottered
on its foundations; the monarchy was threatened by massive subversion,
and it was the hour for the nobility to shake off its collective lethargy and
defend its rights and its Prince. . .

Essentially, the King decided to reprimand the astonishing bravado
of the Third Estate by a powerful gesture. Mr. Necker, seeing the rapid
progess of the development he had initially welcomed, advised him to use
all his authority. He was the first to suggest measures he would later dis-
avow. On 20 June, after a fanfare, the Herald at Arms published a Royal
Proclamation announcing that His Majesty had decided to hold a Séance
Royale at the Estates General. This would take place in two days time and,
in order to allow the necessary preparations in the three assembly rooms,
the Orders were suspended until then. The Grand Master of Ceremonies
wrote directly to Mr. Bailly to inform him of the King's plans. . . (*Confusion*
over arrangements led to the Tennis-Court Oath of 20 June, whereby the
Assembly swore not to disperse until a constitution had been established)

(*Following the storming of the Bastille on 14 July*), the insubordinate
example set by the capital was only too faithfully imitated in the provinces.
The spirit of revolt against the sovereign, and hatred of the nobility, clergy
and magistracy, appeared almost spontaneously from one end of the kingdom to the other. It was like being back in barbarian days, as groups of
frenzied peasants behaved like wild beasts, attacking anyone unfortunate
enough to have been born a gentleman (these attacks were called by the
name 'jacquerie'). . .

The Assembly had long been deaf to the pitiful cries of a nobility
decimated by assassinations and plundering. It ignored the violence that
some of its members had dumbly provoked. Finally, the excesses multi-
plied, burnings became daily more frequent, threatening to envelop the

land with ashes. Something had to be done to shake off this disgraceful apathy, to remedy the intolerable situation so damaging to our reputation. The deputies united in favour of a declaration to be published all over the kingdom.

2

Necker to the King, following the latter's note dismissing him as minister. Roland cote.359

11 July 1789

Sire,

Your Majesty is losing his most tenderly devoted and honest servant. Please have fond memories of me. I hope you would allow me to justify myself if you have any doubts. Sire, I lay before you all these feelings which are engraved upon my heart. I am leaving alone, without passing through Paris, or talking to anyone. I ask Your Majesty to be similarly discreet.

Necker

3

Necker to the King, on hearing of his reappointment as principal minister following the Parisian uprising of 14 July

Basle,
23 July 1789

Sire,

I was reaching the haven that so much agitation had made me wish for, when I received the letter with which Your Majesty has honoured me. I will return to your side to receive my orders, and judge at first hand whether through my toil and unstinting devotion I can again be of service to you. I believe you wish me to return since you have deigned to ask me, and I know your good faith. But I beg you also to believe me on my word when

I say that I am no longer charmed by the seductions that lead men to seek high office. Without a sense of virtue and dignity for the King's esteem, I could have nourished my feelings of love and involvement in Your Majesty's glory and happiness only in solitary retreat...

Necker

4

Note from Lafayette, December 1789. Written out in the King's hand. Roland cote.359

However difficult our circumstances, we can and must prevail. But we have no time to lose, and cannot neglect any means. The only chance for the safety of the nation and the King that I can go along with is the establishment of a free constitution based on the general interest.

The king can no longer waiver between the parties. On one side is the debris of an impotent aristocracy, always taking and never giving. On the other side is the entire nation which ensures Your Majesty's glory, goodness and power. Necessity and the King's wishes must decide whether he abandons any idea of a return to the old regime, and rallies everyone around the national standard. The King must take the offensive against any illiberal or anti-constitutional ideas. Even his courtiers must understand that in a free country his role is to be a man of the people.

The King's council must unite in a firm alliance of its members. Such solidarity will be vital for their safety and power. Every measure must be discussed and decided upon in committee. Far from encouraging a polemical rivalry among themselves and the National Assembly, the Ministers, in all conscience, must work with the Assembly and show it respect. They should keep, however, a certain distance and dignity in their deliberation of affairs.

As for the Assembly, its members must cooperate with the executive for the common good, and learn to curb the vanity, faction and high-spirits which have caused a loss of reputation and time. They must not forget that the people do not want a Long Parliament here, but must be zealous in carrying out the functions of a Constituent Assembly (*i.e. to form a constitution*). Acts of pure legislation should be left for an ordinary and better-balanced legislative.

I therefore propose:

1. that the Court gives up any appearance of constraint and discontent, and that great care is taken to watch over anything which might give hope or power to the enemies of liberty and regeneration, as well as the Orleanist faction, such as military matters, diplomatic developments, interior details of the Palace, and information on plots and exemplary punishments.

2. that a committee of the principal ministers meets twice a week to discuss ways of perfecting the Revolution, of safe-guarding the law, of guaranteeing national security at home and abroad, of sharpening the resolve of the executive... The Committee's first job will be the establishment of a national agency for food supply.

3. that a committee of influential members of the Assembly is formed to regulate and hasten this work. I think the Assembly should be working on the creation of municipalities and provincial assemblies that will place administrative bodies under the government's direction, and will give them impetus from the moment they come into force (*following the introduction of departments, municipalities, etc*).

5

Petition from the mayor of Versailles to the King, on the transformation of the city following the court's move to Paris in the journées of 5-6 October 1789. Roland cote.473

Versailles,
14 April 1790

I beg you to forgive me for being so bold as to write to you directly regarding a matter of the greatest importance... Sire, I am unaware, especially at present, of the extent of remediary measures. But the proofs of your generosity towards your people, and of your special relationship with this town,... are all around me. These proofs lend me the courage I need to present to your generous heart an account of the present grievous situation...

It is impossible to hide the truth of the matter. The withdrawal of the Court and the offices attached to it, has reduced the majority of the town's inhabitants to a dreadful state and numerous day-labourers are without work and bread. Artisans and even some of the artists have found that the lack of work has forced them to seek jobs on the Canal project. There are many who were not directly employed by Your Majesty who nevertheless were dependent upon him for their jobs— tailors, pastrymakers, clockmakers... The crowd of unfortunate people who besiege my door every day asking for bread, greatly exceeds the number of those who have gained work on the Canal...

> Coste
> Mayor of Versailles,
> First Physician
> of the Armies

<hr>

6

Petition from a cleric formerly preacher in the Court, attacking religious and constitutional reforms introduced by the Constituent Assembly. Roland cote.4

3 May 1790

I the undersigned, Claude Louis Rousseau, preacher of the Royal Household, honorary abbé at Lure abbey, Vicar-General of Ably and Canon of Chartres, feeling the most profound respect for the Estates General convoked by the king and constituted by the bailliages and sénéchaussées of the kingdom, in order, together with the supreme head of the state, the monarch, to work for the re-establishment of financial stability, for an equal and proportional tax burden on all citizens, for the reform of all types of abuses, for the elimination of vices and errors that might have affected the ancient and precious French Constitution, and finally for the return of all members of the clergy, be they secular or regular, to a complete and proper observance of the holy canons and rules of the church, an observance as necessary in political relationships as in those of Religion; I was personally involved in the bailliage of Chartres and, by proxy, in the sénéchaussée of Forcalquier, in the making of the general cahiers.

Today, using the incontestable privilege given me by my status as an elector, to examine whether our representatives have thus far been faithful to the task of forcefully carrying out our wishes as we expressed them, it is with great distress that I see that several of the decrees of the National Assembly, no doubt against its intentions, strike a most cruel blow against the sacred rights of Religion, Justice and Property, against the Constituted Principles of the Monarchy, against the exercise of the true and legitimate power of the prince, and against the liberty, the safety and the happiness of the people. Before my conscience and honour, beneath the gaze of God the incorruptible judge, I declare that as a Frenchman and a subject, as a citizen and a priest, I feel obliged to protest, and I do so, against the decree which, taking from the King his inalienable and imprescriptable rights to be a free and essential part of the legislative process, only gives him a suspensive veto (*11 September 1789*); against the decree which refused to acknowledge the Catholic, Apostolic and Roman Religion as the only religion of the State (*13 April 1790*); against the decree which abolished the tithe without compensation—when previously a majority had definitely recognised and decided that some sort of replacement would be fair; against the decree which puts the wealth of the clergy at the disposal of the Nation (*2 November 1789*); against the decree allowing a general invasion of ecclesiastical revenues, and the absolute despoilment of titularies (*4–11 August 1789*); against the administration by which the municipalities and departments are trying to take over our goods (I reserve the right to demand complete restitution of everything that is taken from me by violence, when the laws regain their empire); against the total destruction of all the courts, whose members are to be thrown out of office despite not having been convicted of nor blamed for any punishable crime; and finally against all that has been done in the National Assembly, either opposed or harmful to the maintanance of religion, to the majesty and solemnity of public worship, to the discipline of the universal church in the kingdom, to the hierarchy and dignity of the Holy Ministry, to the just prerogatives of the Crown, to the power of the sovereign, to the standing of France in Europe, and to the inviolability of the legitimate possessions of all citizens...

I protest no less strongly against the incredible silence kept by the National Assembly on the subject of the horrible crimes committed on the dreadful 'journées' of 5 and 6 October last year, crimes which cover France in an eternal and irredeemable ignominy...

I am convinced that the offers made in the name of the clergy by several of its members in the National Assembly, offers to contribute effectively and quickly to relieving the kingdom and paying off the public debt, would have saved the state without involving any of the inconveniences attached to the destructive system adopted instead. In my soul, I adhere to these offers and, in order to do everything possible in my power to make a successful outcome more likely, I pledge that I will receive only half my income for the next four years, or as long as the situation necessitates.

In concert with all good citizens and true French people, I dare to express to my august and unfortunate sovereign my desire to see the kingdom regenerated; for the people to enjoy a wise and generous liberty protected by the law, under the shadow of the throne; for them to be able freely and voluntarily to offer the monarch proof of their love for his sacred person and of their attachment to their country... I will never cease to demand, solicit and urge the wholesale adoption of the frank and loyal declarations made by His Majesty on 23 June 1789 as perfectly in harmony with the spirit, customs and character of the French Nation, and as the most faithful expression of the cahiers of the different bailliages...

7

A further ecclesiastical petition to the King. Roland cote.5

This day, 4 May 1790, the Ecclesiastical Chamber of the Diocese of Toulouse, assembled in one of the rooms of the archbishop's place, having taken cognizance of the decrees of the National Assembly relative to the state and property of the clergy, considering that in sacrificing the tithes which formed the principal endowment of the churches in this diocese, without any equivalent replacement, the deputies to the Estates General have obviously compromised the existence of the clergy, and violated their mandate; that they have made a solemn promise at the foot of the altar to maintain all legitimate property; that it is not enough to extricate oneself from an oath made in front of God by simply declaring that one has ceased to be faithful to him, and that no power, no human consideration can, nor will be able to legitimate such a forbidden abandonment; that the invasion of the fundamental property of the clergy is a crime against the unvarying principles of morality and equity, and that force and violence cannot in the long run prevail against Justice...

To take from the clergy lands and wealth which were given neither by nor for the Nation, but to the churches, priests and the poor for public service under a guarantee from the nation protecting the ownership of each individual and community, is to violate a sworn oath, to deny the wishes of the Church's founders, to ravage the possessions of families, and to ride roughshod over human conventions by breaking the bonds linking and uniting citizens...

To reduce ministers to a monetary salary and—we are not afraid to say—an uncertain and precarious salary is to hand over the Catholic religion to the hazard of events; that this holy religion has only one faith, one worship and one morality, and the refusal to declare it the religion of the state and to preserve for it the monopoly of public faith, tends towards nothing less than to destroy it in the kingdom by introducing confusion between dogmas, sects and cults...

Along with other beneficiaries of donations from the Church, the poor are fundamentally interested in its survival; the destruction of the Church's wealth is a disastrous blow to the patrimony of the poor and to the resources put aside by founders—in spite of the rantings of philosophy and the evil rumours designed to discredit the clergy, the poor have never enjoyed such abundant and regular aid as that they receive from this patrimony, which is like a nest-egg they can discover in their hour of need...

To destroy the monastic institutions that are so dear to the Church in such an indiscriminate and illegal fashion is to show a complete lack of awareness of the respect owed to them...

8

Letter from Boisgelin de Cucé , archbishop of Aix and deputy in the Constituent Assembly, concerning discussions in the Assembly on the Civil Constitution of the Clergy. Roland cote.33

12 June 1790

Sire,

I am taking the liberty of sending to Your Majesty a speech, which recalls the rules of the councils of the church and the laws of the kingdom, the conclusions of which are supported by nearly all the bishops in the National Assembly. We ask for the observation of canonical forms, and the meeting of civil and ecclesiastical authorities. We have reason to believe that the Assembly will ask Your Majesty to take the steps necessary for the execution of its decrees (*under which the corporate organisation of the church would be abolished*). It will then be up to your authority, Sire, to maintain the bonds between the Gallican Church and all other churches, and notably with the head of the Universal Church, the centre of Catholic unity. The Gallican Church has preserved the precious forms which support its constant doctrines and liberties, which signify the enforcement of rules, and leave nothing to fear from the influence of a foreign power. It is with confidence that we submit these useful forms to Your Majesty—they can alleviate difficulties, and conciliate between the laws of the state and the discipline of the Church whose protector and disciple Your Majesty has always been.

Extract from the speech

We respectfully ask the King and the representatives of the Nation first to permit the convocation of a National Council to work in the presence of commissioners named by His Majesty towards the correction of the abuses into which the clergy has slipped, and the re-establishment of ecclesiastical discipline, and to advise on means to conciliate between the interests of religion and the spiritual health of the people, and those of the civil and political spheres of the Nation.

9

Necker's note to the King, following demonstrations in Paris criticising the ministers shows the minister's increasing despondency. He resigned 4 September. Roland cote.603

3 July 1790

Sire,

Your Majesty knows about yesterday's events, but I do not know whether you have been told that an aide-de-camp of Lafayette's came to advise me to take refuge in a friend's house. He added that a detachment of troops would be placed at the Treasury and that a crowd which gathered at the house of Mr. La Tour du Pin (*War Minister*) had stated its intention of regrouping at my house. I decided to leave Paris. My wife, however, is in a very delicate state of health, and my worries for her threaten to make me ill. I agonised over my decision, and also whether I should write to the National Assembly... You know that for a while now I have needed to get away. At the moment I am too anguished to write or to tell you of my true feelings. So poorly is my state that I am not doing everything that I should to acquit my duties to Your Majesty and the state.

Necker

10

Diplomatic missive from Pope Pius VI, concerning the Civil Constitution of the Clergy, discussion of which had been going on for several months, and which was decreed on 12 July 1790. The Pope did not make his opposition public until March 1791. Roland cote.23

Rome,
9 July 1790

We have no doubt, dear son, of your attachment to the Catholic Apostolic and Roman religion, to the centre of unity, to the Holy Seat, to ourself and to the faith of your glorious ancestors, but we fear that for specious and illusory reasons, your love for your people and your ardent desire to see the return of peace and order in Your Majesty's kingdom are being abused. Vicar of Jesus Christ, charged with safeguarding the Faith, we must not enlighten you concerning your duties towards God and your people;... but we must tell you with firmness and paternal love that if you approve the decrees concerning the clergy you will lead your whole nation into error, you will throw your nation into schism and perhaps into a cruel religious war. We have been scrupulous in not inciting such a war, using until now only the innocent arms of prayer. But if religion continues to be threatened, we will be obliged, as Head of the Church, to make our voice heard, without jettisoning the rules of charity. We owe much to the world, Sire, but still more to God.

Do not believe that a purely political body *(i.e. the National Assembly)* can change the doctrine and universal discipline of the Church, despise and count for nothing the feelings of the Holy Fathers and the Councils, and destroy the hierarchy; nor that it can legislate on the election of bishops, or the suppression of episcopal seats, in a word, disfigure the entire organisation of the Catholic Church by changing it to its own liking.

Your Majesty has made the greatest sacrifices for the good of the nation; but if he has renounced certain prerogatives attached to the crown, he cannot under any circumstances sacrifice what he owes to God and to the Church of which he is the eldest son...

From all our heart, we send to Your Majesty and your family our paternal and apostolic blessing...

Pius VI

11

Letter from Cardinal de Rohan, archbishop of Strasbourg, protesting against the Civil Constitution of the Clergy. Virtually all Ancien Régime bishops did the same. Roland cote.1

23 November 1790

Sire,

The most profound respect obliges me to lay before the throne the sadness and regret I have in being forced to protest against the decrees sanctioned by Your Majesty. For I would not be carrying out my duty if I were to adhere to decisions which undermine the general discipline of the Church and upset its order. All these changes have been decided upon only by the secular power without the agreement of ecclesiastical authority.

It is to the Most Christian King, to the eldest son of the Church, that I address my complaints, and from whom I implore support for all the clergy of Alsace, in particular the Cathedral Chapter of my church. Both these groups, as well as my own seat, recognised and freely submitted to the sceptre of the Kings of France. Certain treaties guaranteed by the European powers, and by you, Sire, assured us peaceful possession of our privileges and the maintenance of the state of religion at that time. However, we are now stripped of our rights; our property is seized; the general proscription includes both the forms of our administration and those of our original constitution; our chapters are suppressed along with our churches and monasteries; they are systematically despoiled of ornaments destined and consecrated to the pomp and majesty of the faith, most of them gifts from the glorious Louis XIV.

Essential changes are being made in the general and specific disciplines of the Church; the order of jurisdictions has been inverted. It is in the name of the nation that such illegal enterprises are openly put into operation: the civil and ecclesiastical courts face destruction without any consideration being given to their sacred titles of establishment and rightful jurisdiction. The nobility has also been stripped of its own existence by being deprived of the property and prerogatives guaranteed to it by the same treaties that we invoke together.

Sire, after such details of the grave and vexatious measures taken against our Holy Religion, I hope Your Majesty accepts that it is also my overwhelming duty to address such protests to the Imperial Diet (*of the*

Holy Roman Empire), now meeting to assess complaints made by princes, institutions and individuals under the treaties guaranteeing their rights and possessions. Moreover, as a member of the Empire, I must more specifically solicit its intervention in respect of Your Majesty.

Having rapidly sketched our misfortunes, I must again respectfully explain that it is with great regret that I present a picture of the painful and grievous situation of the very subjects for whom you feel so strongly. We would like Your Majesty, free from pain and worry, to enjoy all the satisfactions to which his virtues should give him the right.

> I am with great respect,
> Sire, your humble and obe-
> dient servant and subject
> Cardinal de Rohan.

12

Memorandum. On the top, in the King's hand, a note: 'Plan of M. Mont. z., or Monot. z.t.' (=Montmorin?) Enclosed with a letter to the King from Laporte, Intendant of the Civil List, 23 February 1791. Plans for the king's escape from Paris were being actively considered, four months before the flight to Varennes. Roland cote.223

The King's dignity, safety and popularity must be reconciled with the monarch's interests and public tranquillity. Thus, we think any plans seeking to spirit away the king furtively or to secure his escape by force of arms must be rejected at present.

There is no point in going into detail on the secondary ways in which we can win the people to our side. We are trying not only to reawaken people's love for their King, but also to make them consider and pity the plight of Louis XVI, to inspire them to want him restored. The people must want a return to order; the King's declaration of 23rd June *(the royal declaration of reform issued at the Séance royale of 23 June 1789)* will be portrayed as uniting the national will with the real interests of France.

We are sure of the position of the two main faubourgs of Paris, and the strength of our influence there; it is such that another 200,000 livres will produce results in about two weeks. These districts have begun to agree not to follow any demonstrations without our agent's approval. Our initial intention is to pay them to be peaceful.

Having got this far, the King should go riding several days running, and follow the routes we will give him. We will arrange for people to shout 'Long live the King!'. His Majesty can exploit this easy popularity by chatting with the people. If anyone asks him about the distresses of the workers (and this will be arranged), His Majesty should reply 'I have always done everything asked of me by my people, and I have always sought its happiness...'. This action by His Majesty will take place at walking pace, for that will appear less affected than stopping. Finally, the King will throw 20 louis into the crowd, and ride off, saying 'I wish I could do more'.

If such events happened two or three times, the bulk of opinion would be in our favour. Then, the King will discontinue his outings on the pretext of ill-health. We will then take charge of investigating the cause of this indisposition, and turn this to our advantage. We will then require additional aid to take more drastic steps.

There exists a society that may be useful to us. (*Probably the reactionary Club monarchique organised by Malouet and Clermont-Tonnerre*). Poorly organised, it has failed to make the progress that might have been expected of it. But the people will not forget that it has made several free distributions of bread. This society will re-assemble, and on the same day receive a petition from the faubourgs. The petition will discuss whatever events may have arisen by then, but the King's name will not be mentioned. That very day, by demonstrating principles that conform to those suggested in the Declaration of 23 June, the Society will plant in the minds of the capital's inhabitants roots all the stronger for appearing to be impartial.

The day after this session, the King's health being no better, His Majesty will tell the Mayor of Paris that he needs to breathe fresh air for a few days. This letter must be carefully phrased, as our allies will write a commentary on it. The absence the King requests must be no more than eight days.

The Mayor's response (in concert with the Assembly) will no doubt be to authorise a few walks at Saint-Cloud. Then our full plan comes into operation.

It is noticeable that when the dominant faction finds itself in contradiction with the decrees of the Assembly or the fixed laws of justice, disaffected groups of people gather together, the atmosphere in the Paris sections heats up, and in a matter of two or three days a deputation or an insurrection motivated by the safety, or just the simple will, of the people, allows the enemies of liberty, France and the King to win an easy victory. Consequently, the morning after the King's letter to the Mayor is made public, a crowd of *our people* will go to the Palace at 6 a.m. and demand to speak to the King. A deputation, more respectful and less frightening than that of 5 October, will press the King not to delay his departure and endanger his health. His Majesty will say that he is afraid to do anything that will give his opponents the pretext further to slander him unjustly, and he can point out how badly he has been treated. The reply from the deputation will convince him that we have given the people all the right ideas. Versailles has too many unpleasant associations for the King, and his safety might be compromised there. Saint-Cloud and Rambouillet are too near. The Jacobins have numerous affiliates there. Compiègne and Fontainebleau have the right combination for the health, choice and safety of the King, and he will be urged to choose between these two. The King, without giving his choice, will appear touched by these arguments, and will promise to abide by his people's wishes *if circumstances allow it*. The people, which knows no obstacles to its wishes, and is expedient in its means, will say that nothing must stop the King... He can mount his carriage at once, and his people will escort him to the city gates. Two carriages will suffice for His Majesty and his family; the servants can follow later. That is what the people will say, and the King will at once give way.

Up to this point the King is not compromised. He has been seen quite unaffectedly in the faubourgs two or three times, but has not stopped there. His wish for a change of air for a few days is neither new nor unusual; it has been expressed several times before. As for the people's deputation, he has given in to receiving so many different other types that he thought he could not refuse it access. And, in truth, no-one could slander its mission, for it had not been suggested by any popular movement.

Once outside the city, the King may appear more exposed than before, and there are precautions it will be necessary to take in advance... Two things must be considered; the speed of the voyage, and the King's safety.

The sooner the King is outside the walls of Paris, the sooner the crown will be back on his head. Acceptance of the Declaration of 23 June, which summarises the reciprocal duties of the throne and the nation must be the aim of the efforts of the King and his supporters...

We submit our plan for your careful consideration. If it needs modification, we will argue this out with the person who will revise it; but as the first phase is neither costly nor likely to compromise anyone, we could at least put it into operation if we are given the initial 200,000 livres. Two or three conversations will suffice to iron out uncertainties and fill in the gaps.

Note : we have some secondary means for swaying the people. They are:

the workshops and their owners
a large number of writers
numerous spies
several former corporations, e.g. the bazoche (*legal clerks*)
the Society of the Faubourg Saint-Antoine, which will do whatever we suggest.

13

Letter from Laporte, main source of pro-governmental secret patronage. Roland cote.221

2 March 1791

Sire,

When I told Your Majesty this morning of the conversation I had yesterday with Mr. de Luchet, I didn't expect to hear what I had thought to be the most secret part of the visit discussed openly so quickly. I received the enclosed two hours ago.

The demands are pretty clear. Mr. Mirabeau wants a guaranteed income in future, either in a life bond from the Treasury, or in property. He has not fixed a sum. If it were a question of negotiating this at the moment, I would suggest that Your Majesty favours the life bond.

But the main thing I would like today is to know what I must do about approaching Mr. L.... *(Lameth?)*

Do you approve of me seeing Mr. M... *(=Mirabeau)*? What are the limits of what I can tell him? Should I sound him out on his plans? What guarantees of his conduct should I ask for? What should I promise him now, and what for the future? If this relationship requires shrewd conduct, Sire, then even more it needs frankness and good faith. Mr. M. has already been wronged —I'm sure he said that Mr. Necker snubbed him twice last year.

Further I'm convinced that he is the only man who can really be useful to you in the present circumstances. He is an angry man, who feels very strongly opposed to the Triumvirate (*the constitutional monarchists*

Barnave, Adrien Duport and Lameth who dominated the Paris Jacobin Club and the Constituent Assembly). We must pick our moment, and make him act in such a way that he can never be reconciled to its members.

The other paper I am sending you is about the deserter from the Soissonnais regiment—it could be very useful in our plan to dissolve the clubs.

I am your humble and obedient servant and subject,

Laporte.

14

Letter from Laporte. Roland cote.220

3 March 1791

Sire,

I cannot see Your Majesty this morning, as I have to hold a meeting of the commissioners investigating Your Household. I enclose two reports, one from yesterday and today's.

A split has developed between Mr. de M*(irabeau)* and the leading Jacobins. It appears they have decided to push him to the limit, in the hope of frightening him into submission. All we have to do is sustain Mr. de M. in his own resolution to sabotage the work of these fanatics.

I will come tomorrow to receive Your Majesty's orders. I beg you to receive my assurances of my devotion and deep respect.

Laporte

Note from Louis XVI to the bishop of Clermont. The latter was a well-known reactionary and opponent of the Civil Constitution of the Clergy. Not dated, but probably 16 April 1791, just preceding the king's abortive attempt to leave Paris for Saint-Cloud where he could receive Easter communion from a non-juring priest, and from where he might also flee. Roland cote.12

I am confidently consulting you, my Lord Bishop, as one of the clergy who has consistently shown the most enlightened zeal for religion. I am writing to you on the subject of my Easter duties. Can I, or must I, perform them in the next fortnight? You know how unfortunate it would be if I give the appearance of being forced into them. I have never hesitated in remaining at one with Catholic pastors in my own affairs. I am also firmly resolved fully to re-establish the Catholic faith if I recover my power. One priest I have seen thinks these feelings are sufficient, and that I can go ahead with my worship. But you are better placed to know what the Church thinks in general, and in the particular circumstances in which we find ourselves. If, on the one hand, this would not scandalise one group, I see, on the other hand, innovators (who are, in truth, not to be counted on) already talking menacingly. Please see those bishops you think fit and whose discretion you are sure of. I would also like you to reply tomorrow before noon, and to send me back my letter.

Louis

Draft of a speech or declaration in Louis XVI's hand. Undated, but probably from the spring of 1791. Roland cote.21

In accepting the decree on the Civil Constitution of the Clergy, the King had it announced that he would take, in his wisdom, the necessary measures to ensure its execution. Consequently, His Majesty has written two letters to the Pope to obtain from him a consent capable of resolving any problems of conscience. While waiting for a reply, the new decree has been presented to him. His Majesty considers this matter to be of the highest importance, and thinks that undue haste could have the most disastrous

consequences through the schism and the internal troubles that might result, consequences which he knows that the Assembly is as anxious to avoid
as he is. Therefore, His Majesty wishes to inform the Assembly that while
he has suspended execution of the decree, he is doing everything to hasten
a decision from the Pope, including sending another courier with urgent
instructions, the results of which will be passed on. His Majesty hopes that
the Assembly will confidently agree with him that the execution of the law
is entrusted to him by the decrees, and that by taking calm but steady
steps he intends to reaffirm the basis of the Constitution of the Kingdom.

17

*Draft memorandum in the King's hand. Marginalia: 'Plan, 11 August'
(1791) and 'abbé de M.' Roland cote.406*

Gentlemen,

I am going to examine the Constitution you have sent me. Like
you, I have felt the need for a revision which, by clarifying on my part
all ideas of constraint, will leave no uncertainty over the stability of the
new laws. This was the purpose of my trip to Montmédy. *(the flight to
Varennes)* I had to escape my captivity, even at risk of war; I had to get
away from Paris so that Royal Majesty would no longer be abused; I had
to reach the provinces, so that I could learn their views, throw factions into
confusion, and, by separating myself from all classes, make a statement to
the whole nation.

I wished to say the following:

"For two years you have experimented with a new form of government.
I have accepted all the new laws, so that they can be tested by experience.
Let us learn from that experience today as we review our Constitution,
by ceasing to allow faction to divide us, and by sacrificing our individual
desires on behalf of the Nation, as I have just done. This was the purpose
of my trip to Montmédy. My opponents, however, have made an evil out of
the most virtuous act of my life. They have separated my happiness from
that of the people, and all my sworn allies have been declared criminals.
Without even thinking how the national interest has been compromised,
they show scant disregard for the personal discomfort they have caused
me. By questioning my intentions they have alienated me from the public
support I need. Whatever cross I am made to bear, I will never be forced

to betray my duties. The people may be unjust, but I will not betray its cause, and will dredge my soul to find the freedom to defend it."

The speech could end here, but in case I'm asked to express the idea in another way, I will put it down here.

"I am trying to call to my side people whose talents will be useful to me in this great undertaking. If it is true that foreign invasions are endangering this, then I will speak out; I will call on my people, march at its front to repel the enemy, and then, having restored the nation to order and peace, I will re-examine the Constitution. One wish is constant—to ensure the same peace inside France that we have won abroad."

18

Undated memorandum, in the King's hand, probably from July or August 1791. Roland cote. 407

27 July 1791

Of all the dangers that have surrounded the King, I fear one in particular if it is prolonged. That is the mistrust felt by the people of His Majesty's character and intentions. If the King were to accept the Constitution unconditionally, it would be said that his latest oath would be retracted like his first as soon as he felt secure. Thus such an acceptance, far from reassuring the French people, would only increase their mistrust. The King would needlessly forfeit his esteem at home and abroad. It must not be feared, however, that he will so easily abandon his dignity, whatever the motives others attribute to him. On the other hand, it would be even more dangerous to give an absolute refusal to the Constitution as it stands. In a less critical situation the King of Sweden offered his crown to the Estates, but he still had strong support in the Diet, and his opponents had nothing much to gain from his abdication. By contrast, in France, the majority in the Assembly would not be able to fail to perceive that a refusal by the King was a symbol of his decline. The republican party, made up of so many factions, would gain new momentum, while the king and his family could only fear even greater misfortunes. Not even his voluntary abdication would ensure his freedom. Thus he must take up a position between these two extremes of refusal and acceptance, in order to preserve his dignity, minimise danger and leave no pretext for rumour and gossip. When the Constitution is presented to him, the King must say roughly the following:

"Gentlemen, it has always been my belief that I have a right to have a say in the kingdom's constitution. For I too am a representative of the Nation, and my interests are inseparable from its. The first wish of the people was that we should settle the articles of the Constitution together. In the national interest I must be able freely to consult with you. But my first duty, and most ardent wish, is to prevent trouble in my kingdom. If you wish to debate on my remarks, I insist that you also consider my declaration of 20 June *(the memorandum left behind by the King on his flight to Varennes)*. If you continue to believe that my acceptance must be unconditional, I will have done everything possible for the general good and for my own conscience. I will not hesitate to declare my voluntary sacrifice of my opinions for the sake of public peace. I would then like to swear irrevocably my loyalty to the Constitution. If it fulfils the nation's wishes then it will also fulfil mine. If, however, experience proved the wisdom of my doubts, I would await for a more enlightened public opinion to make the changes which today appear necessary to me."

19

Undated anonymous memorandum, written in the King's hand, but with the marginal annotation 'Archbishop of Aix'. Roland cote.417, 404

One must give advice both when one is aware of the situation, and where circumstances seem to make advice impossible.

There are moments when one can only take advice from oneself. This rule holds for Kings as well as other men in important matters. If the King risks his crown by refusing to accept the Constitution, some people might warn him that he is running the risk, but they cannot make his decision for him.

They say that under the Constitution, Louis is still King; but he is not, for he no longer has royal authority; because he is effectively kept a prisoner, suspended from his functions; because he can only be a King as a judge is a judge having taken the oath...

The legislature will have all the state revenues at its disposal; it will be able to determine the number, state of advancement, and position of troops on land and sea. It will command the administration using the unsanctioned constitutional police. It will pursue ministers and agents of the executive. Distributing rewards and honours, it will dictate negotiations for war and peace, and use the armed forces for internal policy where necessary. It will be convoked by itself, and cannot be dissolved. It will thus have the same power as the present Assembly; and when it announces that it is the constituted body, what force or authority will stop it?

The King will have no power.

What is the king's position? He is consenting to the loss of the monarchy. He is allowing the destruction of religion. He is abandoning the nobility. If we look at the Revolution established in Paris and the kingdom, we must not lose sight of the counter-revolution being prepared on the frontiers...

This is what the safety of the state, the King and the Queen depends on: a general who will rally the armed forces around the throne. Then the party chiefs will be incapable of further action, and their violent insurrection will peter out, leaving us to repair the damage. Then the princes will return without making war and dictating laws, and will take up their former positions under the King's protection. Then the King will be able to choose his ministers in private...

Good government can be summed up in two maxims:
1. advice is useless without strength
2. strength is useless without wisdom...

20

Anonymous, undated document, entitled 'Memorandum containing a plan for monarchical government'. Probably autumn, 1791. Roland cote.397

If the voice of reason can be heard above the squabble of factions, I do not give up hope that peace and good order will return. I think the kingdom is safe, because we have succeeded in preserving the monarchy. Now, all we need is to pull the King out of the abject state into which he has fallen, to give the necessary strength back to his executive power, and to give him the means to check the insubordinate powers created by the Assembly in a moment of madness. The Assembly itself is threatened by this confused mass of independent authorities; they can hardly be said to form a government. In the end they will overthrow the Assembly, as the Assembly overthrew the King. It would be much easier to restore order if people would only understand that revolutions are ended by compromise. The democratic party would have to give up ideas of an imaginary republic, the idea of which can only have come from deranged minds.

Most people want a monarchy. But there also exist exaggerated and incoherent ideas about the form of the monarchy. One group will lead to tyranny, the other to confusion. One would like a despot before whom people kneel and grovel; the other hardly wants a King at all, fearing his power. Thus, we have an extremist government almost by default, and we face the apparent choice between falling into the lethargy of slavery, and living under the convulsions of anarchy.

If I were asked at the moment how we have come to face this alternative, I would say that it is because some people wanted a Revolution when the majority of France wanted only reform.

A Revolution is not only a matter of philosophical calculation; it is also to do with sentiment. Theorising about legislative, executive and judicial power is all very well in books of utopian philosophy, where difficult problems are simply ignored; but it is absurd to think that such theory can be taught to the ignorant multitude—they can hardly run their own lives, let alone deal with abstract ideas. . .

Further, events have constituted not so much a Revolution as a widespread upheaval. It is the individuals employed by the Government, rather than its actual forms, that have been changed. We have seen the work of thieves, greedily dividing up the spoils of their attack on the church and the nobility. No dignity, no grandeur of soul, no generosity has presided over a Revolution undertaken with such mean and criminal motives.

The institutions that have been destroyed were targets because they were seen as barriers to the agents of this great intrigue. Once they were removed, these individuals have carried on with their greedy plundering. Their wickedness in unrivalled in the annals of world history. To call such brigandage a Revolution is to degrade the word.

Some of the innovators have good intentions, but not the majority. In spite of the republican propaganda of a few individuals, the monarchy has survived because the people know in their heart of hearts that it is the form of government that suits them best. They have only ever proclaimed their hatred of abuses, and their love for the King.

In this embarrassing situation, the real issues have been evaded. The monarchy has been destroyed, but royalty is still respected. The throne has been swallowed up, but its image allowed to remain. The result is a hybrid government composed of discordant parts. It is neither a monarchy nor a republican government. Everybody governs but nobody reigns. Those who must obey are strong, the weak are giving orders. If this anarchy continues, we will never be free, and eventually the tyranny of the executive will replace the present tyranny of the legislature.

What can be done to save the kingdom from this dreadful and worsening confusion? Unfortunately there is nothing more to hope from the

National Assembly...It is controlled by factions who see safety in confusion and disorder. Moreover we cannot hope that the left and the right will unite—they are separated by a wall too high to pull down. The oppressed are never reconciled with their oppressors.

Nor do I believe that a new legislature, if there ever is one, would be any better. The very system of elections decreed by the Assembly is a major obstacle to the healthy composition of a legislative body. New arrivals bring with them new interests and passions. It is much better to debate with known people than to struggle against those whose feelings are unclear...

The various administrative bodies are too closely related to the National Assembly for them to be reliable. There are a few honest staff, but the majority belong to one of the factions.

Should any hope be placed in the numerous clubs set up since the start of the Revolution? No public-spiritedness of any sort emanates from them. Because of their capacity to weaken faction, they might one day be useful to the State. At the moment, however, they encourage division among citizens, and are the greatest impediment to the return of peace and order. It is said that the people itself will grow tired of this crazy Constitution...but the 'people' is an indefinable animal, never so disposed to revolt as when there is no particular grievance for doing so...

In my view then, only the King can save France from the state of anarchy into which she has fallen. Only he can silence the factions; only he can raise his majestic head above the mutinous floods and force them back within their course.

This will not be done by adopting a haughty and threatening tone, still less by seeking people's pity. Such language is always unsuited to a ruler. Rather, by explaining with the dignity that must never leave a King, he must win the admiration and esteem of his subjects. Pity is a weak feeling, offering only sighs and tears. Admiration and esteem make enthusiasts and heroes.

I see the cause of the monarchy as won if the issue can be reduced to just one question: whether we will have a monarchy or a republic. All the Assembly's innovations, however much guided by a democratic spirit, do not frighten me...

The King's tone must be firm and moderate; so must his behaviour. Thus, he must not favour any particular interest. He must show himself to be a conciliator, like a father stepping in between hostile children. In particular, he must beware any talk of vengeance for this would be a great obstacle to the future cessation of hostilities. The only mention of any outrage he has suffered must be to say that he has forgotten about it.

21

Draft speech for the King, probably drawn up for him by Montmorin, in August or September 1791, and the basis of Louis's speech in the Assembly accepting the new constitution, 13 September. Roland cote.114

I have examined with great care the Constitutional Act you have presented for my acceptance, an act which will decide the destiny of the Empire. You will soon learn that I had no hesitation over my decision; but I owe it to Europe, the French Nation and myself to explain my motives. I do not intend to lose this opportunity to fulfil one of the most important duties of my reign—it is time that everybody knows what the King wants, to put an end to the mistrust between him and his people. Having heard what I have to say, no-one will dare to doubt the strength of my resolve.

From the beginning of my reign I have felt the love of the people to be the greatest strength of the monarchy; but I also felt early on that the only way to ensure that love was to make the public interest my primary duty. If I thought that the new form of government you have established would cause perpetual conflicts, and if I thought that my refusal *(of the Constitution)* might one day bring prosperity to the state, then that refusal would be a duty and a glory. Whatever dangers might accompany it, I would put my trust in that Providence that watches over Nations and Kings.

The principles of my conduct are less sufficient than the events of my reign to prove that I have always desired the happiness of my people. I had hardly come to the throne when public opinion demanded the restoration of the old judiciary bodies, and I gave them back their offices. The same public opinion helped to choose the ministers in whom I confided my authority. The financial problem originated before my accession in the expenditure on an honourable and necessary war *(the American War of Independence)* which was not sustained by taxation. To solve this problem, I engaged many enlightened citizens in the administration; at the same time, I and I alone, decided to call the Estates General. I also galvanised public opinion by calling for its views, and I gave the commons *(the Third Estate)* double representation. Has my faith in my people's love ever wavered? Or cast doubt upon the alliance of King and People which is the foundation of the Empire's prosperity?

The same motives directed all my efforts to achieve the regeneration of the realm. My cooperation eased your work. I have been closely associated with this moving Federation by which the united French people showed that they were worthy to be happy and free *(the civic festival, the*

Fete de la Fédération, 14 July 1790). Their main feeling then was hope. Although their shared wishes were known to me, these were desired rather than willed...

Since then, disorder has been widespread, and the new authorities have lacked the strength to combat it. Liberty has degenerated into licence; interest groups have formed factions... In such dissension I see only misfortune. I no longer see the characteristics of the General Will.

However, I had to watch over public tranquillity, and I lacked sufficient means to safeguard it. I therefore decided to distance myself from Paris, to protect the state from the dangers threatening it. My primary aim was to get to know the General Will, which I continue to view as a common law. Yet I must add that I intended to conform to it. Had a constitutional act been presented to me before my departure, I would have refused point blank to accept it. This duty would have exposed me to personal danger, but I would have appealed to the General Will. The general disorder to which I could see no end would have been my justification. Since then, you have recognised that a regular authority is the surest guarantee of public freedom and, with your help, order has begun to return. The excesses of the press have been distinguished from freedom of thought. You have paid attention to policy on public assemblies, to the discipline of the army and to deliberation, which is the real power of constituted authorities.

However, your changing conception of your task has encouraged you to present some decrees to me as if they were constitutional. You have even established legal forms to revise these decress, calling on time and experience. Finally, since then, I have witnessed two particular aspects of public opinion I believe to be pre-eminent. Firstly, the support of the majority of French people for your work, and secondly, the desire of that same majority to defend the monarchical form of government and to restore public order.

I accept the Constitutional Act you have put before me. I will ensure its execution by every means in my power. I will take care to defend the Constitution, and to clarify what constitutes a just defence. My conduct will prove to the Nation that its happiness and liberty are very dear to my heart...

22

Anonymous and undated memorandum entitled 'Observations on the speech proposed to the King'—that is, the speech by which he accepted the constitution. Roland cote.241

If the King is seen as the pilot of a ship, it is obvious that the state, which is the ship, sails on seas which are sometimes calm and sometimes stormy and turbulent. This natural image informs us that the pilot must save the ship, and that he must never leave it at any cost. His course must vary with the weather, and follow all the changes in the waves which, although he really rules them, have the power to submerge him. The history of the Kings of France shows that they either sank or were kept afloat by the strong party of the day.

What finances remained *(i.e. on the King's accession in 1774)* were only enough to last Louis XVI to the fifteenth year of his reign. At that point the slightest excuse caused people to fear bankruptcy, and they forced the calling of the Estates General...

Four enemy factions combined in a unique historical combination, to make a Revolution. These factions were:

1. the rump of the Jansenists and the Parlementaires, who wanted to destroy the pious upper clergy

2. the Protestants who wanted to destroy Rome

3. the capitalists who wanted to destroy the clergy's wealth

4. finally, the cabal of philosophers and logicians who wanted to abolish religion and the nobility, and who, having devoured these two victims, turned on the monarchy. This group has greatly aided the other three. If it is not stopped, it will shatter the kingdom or lead to the worst of Republics.

This is what should have been seen in 1789, and if His Majesty had been given proper advice, there is little doubt that he would have renounced the support of the nobility and the clergy, to reign in future in accord with the strong party i.e. by popular acclaim. After all, if the kingdom is to be ruled, the King must reign; the ship must sail, whichever wind blows. When one pillar of support is removed, the monarch must select another. Nobles and priests could do nothing for the King because they could do nothing for themselves. They might have helped the King if they had had the power to harm him, but their submission to the Court, which was a measure of their friendship, was also an index of their powerlessness. The King could not come down on them, without falling with them. All he could do for the nobility was to refuse to sanction the decree abolishing titles, and the Assembly expected that.

At present, His Majesty's position is not too bad. A little bit of skilful application and zeal in the ministries would quite quickly bring him a great deal of authority, if it were not for two major inconveniences which cannot escape attention. Firstly, the émigrés; secondly, the problem of the clubs, and internal and external dangers.

(With regard to the émigrés)...The Princes are probably more seduced by the schemes of the hardline aristocrats who surround them, and by the romantic and heroic situation in which they find themselves, than they are by the foreign powers. How can Artois really be sure of the Emperor and the King of Prussia's true intentions? If, by some extraordinary occurrence, the émigrés were to come back, it seems to me that their predicament would begin the day after they had returned to Paris in triumph. To conquer is not everything, one must then rule; to rule costs money. What will the King do with a nobility needing to be rewarded, with a clergy demanding all its wealth and land back, with the old financial deficit, and nearly two million livres worth of bad notes in circulation? Would he keep a garrison of, say, 200,000 Germans in his lands? The powers of Europe might limit the King's powers even more than they were limited at the time of the Estates General...

His Majesty can only maintain and govern the state by the popular means of a legislative body; but this can be done, and in proportion to the talents of the King's ministers.

As for the Jacobin clubs, which are so numerous across the country, I think it possible that they will have a violent influence on the next legislature, and that they will force a confrontation between the monarchy and their upstart republicanism. I will show, in another plan, how skilful ministers can arm the Legislatures and the departments against the clubs. The peace of the realm and the safety of the King depend entirely on this.

23

Undated anonymous memorandum, entitled "What will become of France, what will become of the King?". Roland cote.263

What will become of France? What will become of the King? These are the sad questions which are constantly asked in all honest hearts, and by all citizens who care about their country and their King. These two can never be separated. Today, when their dangers and misfortunes are shared, they can be separated less than ever. France's lot is so bound up with that of the King that it depends entirely on the decisions he is still free to make...

The past is the most faithful mirror of the future. It is vital to look at what has happened before deciding what to do. Thus, we must examine what courses the King has followed since he came to the throne, and since the Revolution. If we can show that the misfortunes of the King and the country can be attributed to the Revolution, then we will also show that the King cannot change his plans quickly enough...

What should the King do? Three courses are open to him, all of them with drawbacks and dangers. In present circumstances, no plan would be entirely safe, but it is a question of degree.

The first option is to continue the policy of passive obedience which has been followed to date. The second option is to make efficient recourse to the foreign powers. The third option is to place the King's person at the head of the malcontents, and to have him put forward for the nation's approval all the changes which opinion and sense agree upon.

The first plan, nothing but a continuation of the policy followed over the last three years, is sufficiently compromised by its lack of success to date. It depends on the King for two things; patient acceptance of more suffering, and continued attachment to the Constitution. Of these, one appears useless, and the other impossible. More patience on the king's part will only be to his detriment. Instead of disarming the factions, it will harden their resolve. They will push things to the point where the king will be reduced to despair...

Any efforts to make the Constitution work will only embed its many faults more deeply, and strengthen the impossibility of agreement with it...

Sensible people in France and Europe see the merits of the case made by the King in the excellent Memorandum he had sent to the Assembly on 21 June *(at the time of the flight to Varennes)*

Surely His Majesty sees through the sophistry of the Constitutionalists when they blame the state's problems and the failure of the Constitution on the excesses of the Jacobins. The Constitutionalists are more to blame than the Jacobins—it was they who invented the 'metaphysical government' that is the cause of our misfortunes.

24

Anonymous letter written to the king. Roland cote.244

14 September 1791

The King's delay in giving his final approval to the Constitution has reminded me of quite an important idea which had slipped my mind. It seems to me that His Majesty can follow the Assembly's own example by leaving the door open to the modifications and changes that will inevitably be made to the Constitution. Perhaps His Majesty has already had this idea—I hope so. For if the King were to accept the Constitution with no strings attached, he would be met by cries of horror, outrageous rumours and even open resistance whenever he suggested the smallest change. This paragraph might be inserted into an acceptance speech:

"Nothing perfect has ever been created by man. We use our experience to confirm and support the efforts of our feeble reason. Thus, with proud wisdom, the National Assembly itself has put the final touch to its great edifice. It has recognised the fundamental right of the French people to correct and modify the Constitution; as if fearing premature alterations, it has requested a trial period of thirty years. But the Assembly has also presumed that the Legislative can effect constitutional changes, changes proposed and carried out by the nation's representatives. This right would apply to me as well, as I too am a representative of the Nation: it is my duty to watch over the Constitution, to do everything to ensure its smooth functioning, but also to notice any imperfections. Therefore, I accept the Constitution in the same spirit of wisdom and realism as it is proposed by the National Assembly. But I retain the firm belief that I have the right to notice its blemishes, suggest remedies, even to favour its improvement with all the power that the said Constitution gives me."

It seems useless to develop this general idea on the first of my functions, but I must point out that if I accept the Constitution unconditionally I leave myself vulnerable to the slurs of factions and opponents the moment I make any suggestion or take any action.....etc, etc)

Please make whatever use of this idea you like, Sir. I only ask you to remember how Queen Elizabeth of England used the same idea that I suggest when she was young and a prisoner of her cruel sister Mary. Please forgive my verbosity.

Anonymous memorandum. Roland cote.246

30 September 1791

Sire,

As I write, alone, on the important subject of the people's sovereignty, I cannot help reflecting on the present condition of the government and the nation. I am sending you these thoughts, Sir, inspired by your own frankness; but, I often remember how useless my advice was at the time of the opening of the Estates General, when the Assembly needed a firm hand to direct it away from the struggles of the then nascent and timid factions. I hope my current thoughts have a greater success. Times have changed you will say, and we learn from misfortune. I accept that, but feel sure, Sir, that the reason which foresees disasters and the reason which repairs the damage, are equally little understood. Two things must hinder His Majesty's attempts to derive practical policies from the plans submitted to him, and should also stop him from following a particular 'system'. First, memories of a very different order of things from that which now exists. Secondly, the services rendered by a coalition of a number of deputies with ministers during the First Legislature.

Basically, because the King is placed in his exalted position by the nobility, it is only natural that he cannot all of a sudden become detached from the interests, passions and maxims of that order. Things change around us before we change ourselves, because we cannot sufficiently escape the effects of our education. It is no good saying "What would I do if I had come to power differently?". For Louis XVI, the King must define the man. Alexander abandoned the Greeks when he saw himself as King of Persia...

As for the coalition between the group of deputies and the Ministry, I will content myself with the following observations. Messrs. Thouret, Lechapelier, Barnave etc., in giving their advice, can only carry out their tasks and teach the ministers how to hide the defects in the Constitution. They will spend all their time endlessly refashioning it. This is the opposite of the system we need if we are to escape from the present state of anarchy. Besides, as demonstrated by their latest decrees, these men have lost their popularity. They have no sway in the new Legislature, which is dominated by all the clubs, and has been against them from the start. I would add that none of these gentlemen is powerful outside the chamber. Their empire depends on their lungs.

With reference to the latest rejoicing in Paris, and the popular successes of the King and Queen, I would remark, Sir, that the people could be counted on if left to itself. But its actions will only have irritated the republicans, its mood is changeable, and might be given new direction by systematic channelling of the republicans' anger. Popular enthusiasm has no deep roots. I might add that the majority of the aristocracy is as worried as the democrats by the King's acceptance. Divided by motives, they share this feeling.

In a word, the King might tell himself that he must fight against the democrats, aristocrats, the departments, the clubs etc. on behalf of his people; as once the people fought against the intendants, the commandants, all the court and the ministers.

Happy are the kings who can take bitter advice and keep unpopular counsellors. Seeking an agreeable minister, is as inappropriate as wanting one's mistess to be a 'stateswomen'!

26

Anonymous memorandum entitled 'Rough draft of a speech by the King to all Frenchmen, after the ratification of the Constitution. This speech serves for all circumstances, even including invasion by our enemies and by the émigrés'. Autumn 1791. Roland cote.249

If I were a Prince as foreign to France as the Elector of Saxony is to Poland, it would be in vain that the National Asembly offered me its collected decrees. A Constitution based on so many reefs and obstacles would only cause me anxiety. For myself and my descendants I would not presume to accept an Empire without finance, an army without discipline, and an administration abused by political clubs. What kingdom has ever stood up to these three causes of destruction, these principles of death ?

Yet, I am too linked to France by ties of blood and affection. The sight of even immediate anger cannot separate me from her. How can I forget 800 years of common destiny between my family and the Nation, the thirty Kings, my ancestors and my son, and so many faithful people. No, I will stay at the helm of this storm-tossed ship, this ship so full of hopes and fears.

Today I have an opportunity to declare to France and Europe my two fundamental mistakes. The first was to call democracy to the aid of the monarchy. The second was blindly to sanction all the Assembly's decrees.

By my first error I risked the state. Republics have always fallen at the hands of a single man, but I believed that the monarchy would not succumb so easily. Also I thought that the French people would not allow the spirit of faction to draw them away from their love of the crown, or to abolish the very name of the Monarchy.

By my second error, I compromised, I swear, my reason and my character. I compromised my reason because I sanctioned several decrees which offended natural reason, decrees already under review by the Assembly. Also because I sanctioned on 4 February 1790 the making of a Constitution whether suitable or not for this vast kingdom. I compromised my character because I sanctioned decrees repugnant to my spirit and my heart, and against which one day I must protest. I thereby damaged my reputation for frankness, which was my only natural advantage. The double admission I have made here should prove the extent to which I want to be trusted—I could easily have used the excuse of stopping internal divisions to refuse my sanction and stop the Assembly's work. After so many errors and misfortunes, however, I can only express regret, and do my part to ensure that we get rid of the former and ease the memory of the latter.

27

Undated anonymous memorandum. Probably from late 1791. Roland cote. 253

The King and the Kingdom are one. But what is the Kingdom? Since 1789 it has been the assembled representatives of the Nation. Can we hope that the Kingdom will return to its previous form? No, because the people, who previously counted for nothing, have won their legal equality. This makes them happy, instead of unhappy as they were before, because they are now the strongest group, they know their rights and they have taken up arms; because they regard the Constitution as their own achievement; and finally, because the clergy and the nobility have conducted themselves so badly, and have espoused so many foolish plans, that they have justified the abolition of their orders. Does this abolition affect Your Majesty? Not at all. The King stands above everyone in France, according to the law itself. All the elements that make up the Nation are equal in his eyes, and under the law. This was true in the past as well, when the King could make a commoner into a duke. Thus, nobility is nothing more than regulated prejudice, and the ambition attached to the status of nobility diminishes neither the majesty of the crown nor the splendour of the throne. The monarchy has often been threatened by the overweening power or the pretensions of the nobles. They always asked and the people always gave. They impoverished the King, while the people enriched him. They liked the King for his power, while the people loved him in person. Nobles have always played on the vices and weaknesses of Kings in order to profit from them. The people encouraged a good King to be virtuous. They adored him, and rewarded him for his efforts.

As for the clergy, it was never meant to use its divine inspiration to infiltrate the courts, or to scandalise the people by its wealth, its pride and its vices. The Civil Constitution of the Clergy gave it the chance to return to its original state of purity and virtue. Undoubtedly it would have been preferable gradually to reduce the immense wealth of the church. The clergy were only its usufructuaries. If we had declared that this wealth belonged to the Nation, and that the clergy's worldly goods would be less violently distributed between the need to upkeep the churches and the needs of the state, then there would not have been a murmur of protest. The high clergy, who only asked to enjoy their role, would have agreed, and no fanatical reaction would have been inspired. After all, egoism is the central tenet of the priesthood. Having neither wives nor children, priests are only part of the world through their vice or virtue. Those touched by vice—the majority— cried out in complaint. The virtuous minority made no complaint at the sacrifice of their worldly goods.

Has the Civil Constitution caused a schism? No—the territorial reorganisation of dioceses and parishes has been a purely material matter within the authority of the sovereign. Will it lead to a schism? Yes, if the King and the Legislative Assembly, don't get together to stamp out fanaticism, without being too hard on those people led by priests, and without showing any favours to particular faiths among the diversity that makes up the Catholic Church. This problem must be solved with tact, patience, using purely civil means.

Has the King any particular interest in seeing the two orders of nobility and clergy reestablished? No—on the contrary, he should fear any such development...

<hr>

28

<hr>

Memorandum read to the royal council by the comte de Narbonne, War

Minister, 24 February 1792. Roland cote.542

I don't really know that there is anyone so blind not to see what is really going on in France. Public authority means nothing in a country where the law is not obeyed and legitimate powers are not respected. The extent of personal misfortunes is frightening—capital already reduced by reform is cut to one third of its value by inflation. Individual liberty is only weakly protected by public authority, or is openly attacked by fanatics from inquisitorial societies *(i.e. Jacobin Clubs)* which have claimed the right to tyrannise citizens and even magistrates in the name of liberty.

Also, the fact that most of the countries in Europe are her enemies leaves France facing immense external dangers... Only the coalition of her government and all good citizens of the kingdom will save France, the throne and the King.

The major parties in France are the aristocracy, the republicans and the Constitutionalists. They are all pretty clearly defined, and we know their general intentions; except perhaps for the republicans—with them, it is easier to know that they don't want than what they do want.

Although royal power has appeared gravely weakened since 1789, it undoubtedly still has great influence, and could increase that influence so as to determine the outcome of our present circumstances. The republicans can never hope to work harmoniously with the King; they want only to destroy his power. This leaves the aristocrats and the Constitutionalists battling for the King's ear. The former have the advantage of an apparent common cause with the throne... Often, in self-defence, they invoke the name of royalty, which is heard more favourably than theirs, and gives the impression of a devotion which is undoubtedly the virtue of a few of its members, but which is hardly the dominant feeling of the party... For a long time the King has invited them to cede, as he has, to the changes dictated by the will which he himself has called 'national'...

The Constitutionalists are the authors or supporters of an order of things which forbids anything absolute to royal power, and for which the strength of prerogative has been decided upon by principles, and owes nothing to previous practices. The route that has been followed to reach this goal has probably often seemed more shocking to the King than the goal itself. Mistrust of the King's intentions is one of the republicans' most deadly weapons. Using it, they arouse feelings, cast suspicion upon honest actions, raise the Assembly against the King and render royalty even less dear to the unenlightened parts of the Nation, provoking resistance to constituted authorities.

Ideas like those propagated by the republicans are avidly collected by the aristocrats—they present them to foreign powers to oppose the King's official negotiations or declarations, and use them to inflame weak citizens...

Thus, both sides understand perfectly that this state of mistrust is the surest and most effective way to throw France into confusion...Both the most extreme parties share a scandalous conformity; they want chaos, although they hope to achieve very different things after this chaos...At present they are in league to destroy everything.

Either the King nurses deep in his heart a secret support for the aristocrats, that is for the ancien regime, or else he hopes to form a third party along the lines proposed by him before leaving on his journey to Montmédy *(i.e. the royal family's flight to Varennes, 20 June 1791)*; but, in any case, one might think that he is simply not doing enough to prepare for the results of the total disorganisation threatening us because, either through his private conduct or the carelessness and uselessness of the government's actions, he has given a terrible impetus to the two destructive factions that have taken advantage of our excessive faults...Of all the ways to destroy an Empire, none is more infallible than government inertia. The body politic expires when this necessary organ stops breathing.

The King cannot stand at the head of the Nation without showing resolution to brave all dangers and giving a firm impression of his character and courage...

There remains one very important class of society that it is vital to rally to the throne—the property-owning bourgeoisie. Because of their interests, they are pretty indifferent to the form of the government. The only thing they want is the preservation of their possessions. They will rally to whoever will guarantee this. Unless the King places himself on the side of order, renounces his practice of registering protests against the present regime, or at least perseveres by every means in his power to give credibility to the idea that he will preserve everyone's property, it will stay in most of these men's minds that the King does not want to govern and they will attach themselves to other hopes—after all, their fortunes are their only happiness.

29

A letter from the bureaucrat Dufresne de Saint-Léon reveals both the size of the royal Household and the confusion of royal accounting procedures prior to 1789. Roland cote.134

25 February 1792

Sire,

I am pleased to send you the accounts for the liquidation of the King's household, according to the Decree of 6 February.

I have gathered together all the documents which might form the basis of this liquidation. However, I have not been able to fulfil to the letter the requirements of the Decree of 26 May 1791. It has proved fruitless to try to obtain an exact account for the Royal Household in 1750—over one third of contemporary accounts have been destroyed since then; quarterly résumés have been converted into annual statements. These changes have happened somewhat inevitably in the accounting process; but things are further complicated by the fact that our economic definitions now classify as monetary income a whole range of goods which used to be received in kind, so that the office-holder could take a due reward independent of the effects on the accounts. Any attempt to compare receipts can be based only on very imprecise evaluations.

Further, with regard to the financing of the said officers: these were not really worked out until the time when the Household was being reformed.... Consequently, I have divided this account of the two Households into several chapters... The general total will amount to 33,869,840 livres.

Also attached to these accounts, Sire, you will find those for offices reformed after the edicts of 1781 and 1785. Their holders have not been re-imbursed... but the suppression of the privileges attached to the offices makes me think that their case should be put before the National Assembly. The Assembly may well decide that these officers should not stay on the king's personal account; it's a matter of 22,550 livres.

The Assembly wants to proceed with the liquidation as quickly as possible. This initial review is vital to that task. It would be unjust if office-holders were not assured of reimbursement for the capital they laid out in purchasing their offices.

30

Letter of resignation from Bertrand de Moleville, Minister of the Interior, following the dismissal of the comte de Narbonne as War Minister and the King's decision to appoint a 'Patriot Ministry' of Girondins. Roland cote. 563

9 March 1792

Sire,

I have just learned that Your Majesty has named a successor to Mr. Narbonne. Having considered the matter at length, I feel I must offer you my resignation. Your Majesty can well appreciate my motives—you know my feelings and my conduct. You cannot doubt my courage nor my confidence in your justice. Nor will you be surprised at this latest proof of my devotion.

Sire, you know the circumstances under which I am leaving the Ministry; I leave my reputation in your hands. I remain your most humble, obedient and faithful servant and subject,

Bertrand

31

An ecclesiastical petition similar to many received by Louis. Roland cote.44

18 April 1792

Sire,

The Superior of the Daughters of Charity asks Your Majesty to consider the feelings of respect and trust that she has for him, feelings shared by her dying community, and to forgive the latest liberty she is taking; at the foot of the throne, she begs him to save her institution from the destruction threatened by the decree of 6 April *(suppressing religious congregations)* ... We are now at the eve of the execution of this fatal decree, which will at least be quick. But to cap it all, we are also afraid that we will be uprooted from our mother house... in which we have lived for over 150 years. The house is the only refuge for the infirm, the dying, the paralytics who come to us from throughout the provinces and the capital—it also serves people of less advanced age who have become ill in the service of the poor. Together, these make up a considerable number. This is the plight we are in, Sire, though we deserve no reproach. However, our grave has already been dug, and only a miracle can save us. Only God and Your Majesty can intervene by suspending the sanction of the decree (if that can be done). Whatever may happen, we abandon ourselves into his hands, and assure him that in the last moments of our lives our profound respect will remain unaltered,

> From your humble, obe-
> dient servant and faithful
> subject
> Sister Deleau.

32

A similar petition. Roland cote.95

29 April 1792

A community in tears throws itself at your feet, to implore the help of your power against the most unjust activities of the municipality and the departmental directory of Ille-et-Vilaine, sitting at Rennes. Having for a long while struggled against the persecutions of those holding authority in this area; having been deprived of our property and refused point-blank any help; we now find ourselves faced by even greater threats, by the total loss of our establishment and our status.

As if it were not enough to have stolen our possessions and inhumanly to have denied us our means of subsistence for over a year, they now want to take away our last remaining consolation; that is, the priceless privilege of leading a life that leads to our happiness. To tear us away from this would be to leave a deadly barb in our heart, to plunge us for the rest of our days into a well of bitterness and misery that will never run dry. For we have no more means of support left to us in this world.

For what crime are we treated so harshly? Is it that we refuse to elect a new Superior? How can we do so without breaking our vows? We are so irrevocably attached to our station in life according to Your Majesty's rules for this house, and those of the church, that we can neither elect nor consider any other— are we criminals for doing our duty? We cannot believe that we have earned any reproach. For months we have endured terrible food shortages without a moan or a murmur, in the hope that Providence would restore some feeling of human commiseration to the hearts of our persecutors. Now our hopes are abandoned, and God has sent us a new test...

We remain your humble
and obedient servants and
subjects,
The nuns of St George's
Abbey, Rennes.

33

*Anonymous printed ecclesiastical petition against the law of 27 May 1792
introducing draconian punishment for refractory priests involved in civil
dissent. The King was to veto the decree on 19 June. Roland cote.54*

Sire,

In its last few sessions, the National Assembly has been busy with a
repressive law against disruptive priests. Under this heading, however, the
Assembly has confused all those who have not sworn the civic oath.

If Your Majesty cares to examine in public papers the discussions which
preceded the various clauses of the decree, he will clearly see the influence
of the clubs, and also a neglect of the principles of justice and morality.

We will not remind Your Majesty of the reasons why the sensible party
of the clergy, *those whose morals and virtues inspire confidence*, have refused to take the oath required of them. Sire, they have left themselves
open to attack; they have exposed themselves to a persecution which bears
no comparison with their courage. They are resolved to suffer rather than
to betray their consciences...

Your Majesty must consider the idea that in remaining attached to the
Catholic Faith he has added the ministers of the new church to the ranks
of his enemies. The *intolerant* priests have an inconceivable influence in
the Assembly, and have suggested measures that would extend persecution
to your own chapel, hampering the expression of piety. All those who are
sworn to the defence of the throne are being successively distanced from it.
Sire, your current ministers sit in council at the Jacobin Club—they want to
see only republican spies and members of factions surrounding your family.

Aside from such considerations, each clause of the decree is in clear
transgression of the constitution. Corporations have been destroyed, and
the Assembly has just removed the last traces of them by suppressing religious costumes. But by a sudden reaction against principle, it has now
formed a new corporation of non-juring priests, which is distinguished from
other citizens by severe discrimination...

The National Assembly has classified the deportation of non-juring priests as a matter of administrative policy; yet the first article of the Penal Code includes deportation among capital offences. Thus, despite the equality of punishments and rights, deportation can be summarily ordered against one group of French people, but not against others without a guilty verdict from a jury. This difference undermines all principle, Sire, and should not be allowed—it offends the national interest, the Constitution and Your Majesty's own conscience.

It appears manifestly impolitic to make priests feel that they are under pressure both where they have strong influence over public opinion and where their hold is so precarious that it represents no threat. Why risk the principles upon which our new laws rest? It is said that priests encourage people to disrespect the law, and to avoid taxation, that they sow discord among families, and, by their example, lead many uneducated people into counter-revolution.

These false allegations tar all priests with the same brush, and the decree does the same. Such collective measures, Sire, are fundamentally unjust and oppressive. . .

One of the decree's clauses will not escape Your Majesty's notice; the one which allows twenty active citizens to deport a priest from a canton, no matter what the population of that canton, nor whether the priest is popular among the majority of the area's citizens. Twenty citizens!! the number is as small as the corruption the clause represents is great. How easy it will be to find willing accomplices in the perversion of justice. Was the law ever so barbarous? Sire, this cannot be allowed under a just King. Every day the courts of the popular assemblies resound with complaints against the abuse of arbitrary power and *lettres de cachet*—but they themselves are frighteningly arbitrary. . .

They say that the priests who have not adopted the Civil Constitution by swearing the civic oath, have no right to invoke it. This argument can be refuted, Sire, we can use the speeches of the infamous Mr. Brissot: "It is a great feature of liberty that even her enemies come under her aegis ! Liberty is nothing else but universal justice".

Thus, according to Mr. Brissot, the law protecting our liberty and safety, inseparable in a well-governed state, belongs equally to its friends and enemies, and it must serve for both. Constant in the flux of opinion, the machinery of the law cannot have two forms of application.

However this precious equality of all people in front of the law is violated by the decree. Moreover, the Constitution says that "No citizen can be judged on a criminal matter unless the charges are heard before a jury". Sire, as a capital punishment, deportation can only be sentenced for a crime proved in law. What will become of the other clauses of the Constitution if it continues to be applied so arbitrarily to non-juring priests?

Sire, all these arguments make a strong case for the use of Your Majesty's veto. As *'Most Christian King'* you will signal your protection to the religion you profess. As *constitutional monarch* you will prove your firm resolve to maintain justice and liberty for all. As a *virtuous, just and charitable king* you will give way to the strength of your dislike of oppression and injustice. Your strength will disconcert the factions, which are only influential because they have taken advantage of your goodness. Finally, Sire, you will enjoy the happiness that comes from protecting innocence...

34

Report from Laporte, the king's agent. Roland cote.194

2 June 1792

Sire,

Yesterday evening I sent your Majesty two reports from Mr. Dubut de Longchamp. I am not pleased that his advice has suddenly become rather meaningless—for example, what he says concerning Mme. Elisabeth, *(the King's sister)* and the *Ami du Roi* newspaper. I have told him to keep to the point.

The man he has asked to introduce to our secret meeting was to be at his home at 6 o'clock this morning.

Your Majesty will see that he repeats the opinion that I have heard elsewhere that you should use your veto to suspend execution of the decree concerning coloured people.

It is said that the D.D. (= *the duc d'Orléans?*) gave out 50,000 écus the day before yesterday. He intended to cause fright, but if that does not work, to come to an arrangement under which his debts would be paid and he would be exiled.

35

Report from Laporte, the following day. Roland cote.193

3 June 1792

Sire,

The intermediary who brings me reports from Mr. Dubut de Long-champ showed me yesterday evening a letter from Longchamp confirming his trust for his messenger. He also wrote that he did not know how the news was passed to Your Majesty, that he would like to know whether or not the reports were made, and if they were satisfactory. Finally, he asked Your Majesty to receive him.

I had him told that this was impossible—he could not be smuggled into Your Majesty's apartments without being noticed, and this would compro-mise him as well as yourself, Sire. Longchamp has accepted this, and has replied in the letter I attach to mine. You will see for yourself that he now asks you to write him a note to assure him that you know and approve of his work. If Your Majesty agrees to this, and sends me the note, I will make sure it reaches him by Sunday morning at the latest. Longchamp knows your writing—two minutes in possession of such a mark of approval will make him happy.

I also enclose the latest report, full of news I have only begun to take in. There was another set-back yesterday... A demonstration has been called today, but it will not be near the Tuileries. It is aimed at the trial by Santerre of the aide-de-camp which is about to come to an end. There will be a mass lobby of the court—it is reckoned that between 50 and 60,000 livres were spent yesterday to help mobilise the crowd. The Faubourg Saint-Antoine was restless all day.

Longchamp offers to expand on any bits of news that may be unclear to you, and to provide proof if you doubt his facts. The man chosen to introduce him to the infernal committee was at his house yesterday, and was given his instructions.

I think things will change tomorrow. The man above will inform me of events in the meeting, and Longchamp will also make a report. Neither knows that the other is doing this. The reports will be sent to Your Majesty.

36

Letter from Lafayette. Distrusted at court, Lafayette was from his position as commander at the front attempting to intrigue to have his followers appointed ministers following the dismissal of the 'Patriot Ministry'. Roland cote.340

16 June 1792

Sire,

At the moment when I was going to call your attention to matters of great public interest, and include among our dangers the conduct of a ministry I have long been attacking in my letters, I learn that it has succumbed to its own intrigues, unmasked by its divisions. For, without doubt, it is not by sacrificing three colleagues noted for their insignificance to his own power, that the least excusable and most notable of these Ministers will have strengthened his equivocal and scandalous position in the king's Council.

Nevertheless it is not enough that this branch of the government is relieved of a bad influence. The public sphere is in danger, and the safety of France rests principally on its representatives. The Nation looks to them for help, but by giving itself a Constitution, has denied them the one way of saving things.

Gentlemen, I believe that just as the Rights of Man are the laws of any Constituent Assembly, so a Constitution becomes the law for the legislatures it establishes. It is to you, then, that I must denounce the powerful efforts being made to divert you from the rule you promised to follow.

Nothing can stop me from exercising my rights as a free man, or fulfilling the duty of a citizen—neither the transient sway of opinions which undermine principles; nor my respect for the representatives of the People, for I have even greater respect for the People, of whom the Constitution is the Supreme Will; nor, indeed, the good intentions which you have always attributed to me, for I wish to preserve them in the same way I gained them—that is, by the inflexible love of freedom.

Your situation is difficult, France is threatened from outside and within. As soon as the foreign courts announce an intolerable plan to usurp our sovereignty, and thereby declare themselves enemies of France, internal opponents, drunk on fanaticism and the pride of chimerical hopes, tire you with further examples of their insatiable emnity.

They must be reprimanded; and you will only have the power to do this as long as you are just, and keep within the Constitution. No doubt you want this. But look around you. Can you ignore the fact that one faction, the Jacobins to put it bluntly, has caused all the disorder? I accuse it above all. Organised like an independent empire in its metropolis and its affiliated bodies, blindly directed by ambitious leaders, this sect forms a distinct corporation among the French people, usurping its powers by subjugating its representatives and their courts...

Above all, those citizens who have rallied around the Constitution must be assured that the rights guaranteed by it will be respected with a religious faithfulness that will be the despair of its hidden and public enemies. Do not dismiss this wish; it is held by the true friends of your legitimate authority.

37

Letter from Tarbé . The King found it increasingly difficult to find ministers, as anti-monarchical opposition grew over the summer of 1792. Roland cote.440

17 June 1792

Sire

I will never forget the generous way in which you encouraged and supported my efforts. As a Frenchman, I love my King. As a Minister, I have seen at first hand and greatly admired the virtues of Louis XVI. They are deeply etched on my heart.

I hope Your Majesty will deign to listen to the opinions of a respectful and faithful servant. You have just taken an important step, but for it to be successful, it must be carried through. The new ministry must be absolutely new. If a single member is included from the old body, Your Majesty's intention will be greatly compromised. The new Ministry will be judged by the perceived opinions of its predecessor. It is therefore vital that public opinion is made to delay its verdict. During this period of oscillation the Ministry can consolidate its position. Thus, for the public good, I ask you to consider another subject (to be a minister)....

Your humble and
obedient servant,
Tarbé

38

Letter from Roederer, procurator of the department of Paris and an important adviser of the King in the last weeks of the monarchy. Roland cote.531

7 July 1792
4.15 p.m.

The National Assembly has just given the signal for a general reconciliation. The foreign war is giving us internal peace. The general crisis is finally destroying the principles of violent revolution.

Sire, the events of 20 June *(when the Tuileries had been invaded by a Parisian crowd and Louis threatened)* will not happen again, since their cause no longer exists. When the Constituent Assembly thought the Revolution was over, because it said that it was, it announced the abolition of processes of law and decision-making which had already begun. In other words, in the name of the Nation, it withdrew all the complaints of liberty against the guilty supporters of the old monarchy.

Sire, only now is the Revolution reaching its end, for only now is there unity and understanding among the various groups of the revolutionary party. There exists one major complaint held by the name of liberty. This complaint is still debated between two groups, Sire, and could lead to other issues widening the gap between them, eventually leading to a conflict.

Will the Constitutional Monarchy, henceforth totally safe, be less indulgent of the struggles of nascent liberty, than that liberty, itself much less secure, was of the old errors of the previous system of domination and slavery?

Sire, it would be a fine thing if the King of the French was the first to reply enthusiastically to this signal of national reunion. I have taken the liberty of pointing out to Your Majesty what an opportunity this represents for your glory and virtue.

I remain, Sire, your most
humble and obedient ser-
vant,
Roederer.

39

Resignation of Terrier de Montciel, Minister of the Interior since 18 June.
Roland cote.522

17 July 1792

Sire,

I implore Your Majesty to announce to the Assembly that after new attempts by me to obtain my retirement from the ministry, you have given the Interior portfolio to M.Joly. If this is not done this morning, I know that Brissot will propose a motion of impeachment against me.

> I am most respectfully, Sir‹
> your humble and obedi-
> ent servant,
> Terrier.

40

Resignation letter from Scipion de Chambonas, Foreign Minister since 17
June. Roland cote.513

24 July 1792.

Sire,

I have the honour of asking Your Majesty to announce to the Assembly that I have just offered my resignation. I find myself in a position where I am unable to serve faithfully as a minister, but I remain a loyal subject.

The Justice Minister will inform you of what has happened concerning me.

> Sire, I remain your respect-
> ful and faithful servant,
> Scipion Chambonas.

41

Letter from the same. Roland cote 528

Sire,

My health is to my body what the National Assembly is to the King. Though I am no longer your Minister, I will always be a soldier and faithful subject to my prince and master. My allegiance to you, Sire, will never cease. I beg Your Majesty to listen, with the sense of justice for which you are renowned, to what the Minister of the Interior will tell you. It is the truth, as it is true that I would die for the King, or to defend the glory of the French monarchy. Since my birth, I have amply demonstrated my loyalty to the King. If Your Majesty would only acknowledge me, and indicate that he is pleased with me, I will die happy. I beg you to ask the Minister of Foreign Affairs to forward me a portrait of Your Majesty. I don't want gold or diamonds—a portrait is the jewel that will be my most precious possession.

I am, Sire, the most devoted and respectful subject attached to Your Majesty,

Scipion Chambonas.

REFERENCES

Clearly, not all the voluminous literature relating to Louis XVI and his trial can be listed here. For fuller bibliographical guidance, see R.J. Caldwell, *The Era of the French Revolution. A Bibliography of Western Civilization, 1789-99*, New York and London, 1985. Place of publication is Paris (for works in French) and London (for works in French) unless otherwise stated.

Archives Nationales C 183-7

Archives parlementaires, vols., LIII-LVI, XC

A. Aulard, 1889-97: *La Société des Jacobins*, 6 vols.

K. Baker, 1982: 'Ideological Origins of the French Revolution' in D. Lacapra and S. Kaplan, eds, *Modern European Intellectual History*, Cornell

M. Bouloiseau, 1972: *La République jacobine*

Madame Campan, 1821: *Mémoires*

A. Cobban, 1963: *History of Modern France*

C. Desmoulins, 1793: *Histoire des Brissotins*

P. and P. Girault de Coursac, 1982: *Enquête sur le procès du roi Louis XVI*

F. Hue, 1860: *Dernières années de Louis XVI*

D. Jordan, 1979: *The King's Trial*

Journal de la République, 1792-3

102

A. Kuscinsky, 1916–18: *Dictionnaire des Conventionnels*

R. Levasseur, 1860: *Mémoires*

E. Lever, 1985: *Louis XVI*

Le Moniteur, 1792-3

Madame Roland, 1821: *Mémoires*

J. Rothney, 1969: *The Brittany Affair and the Crisis of the Old Régime*, New York

A. Soboul, 1966: *Le Procès de Louis XVI*

M.J. Sydenham, 1969: *The French Revolution*

A. de Tocqueville, 1856: *L'Ancien Régime et la Révolution*

C. Tomlinson, 1853: *The Construction of Locks*

M. Walzer, 1974: *Regicide and revolution*

Printed and bound by CPI Group (UK) Ltd, Croydon, CR0 4YY

13/04/2025

14656587-0003